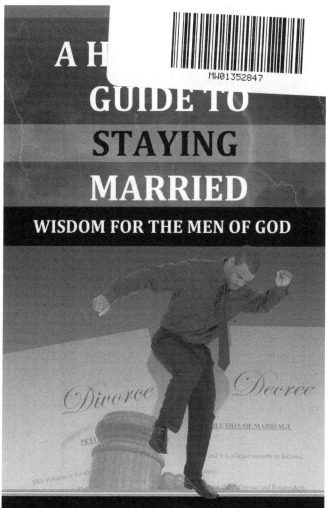

To Molly,
May God bless & keep you always!

A HUSBAND'S GUIDE TO STAYING MARRIED

WISDOM FOR THE MEN OF GOD-ORDAINED

Bishop Ronald R. Mayo

A Husband's Guide to Staying Married
Wisdom For the Men of God

Copyright © 2013
Author Bishop Ronald R. Mayo
Email: info@anointedfire.com

Cover design: Anointed Fire™ Christian Publishing
Publisher: Anointed Fire™ Christian Publishing
Publisher's Website: www.afcpublish.com or
www.anointedfirepublishing.com

All scriptures noted in this book were taken from the King James bible unless otherwise noted.

ALL RIGHTS RESERVED. This book contains material protected under International and Federal Copyright Laws and Treaties. Any unauthorized reprint or use of this material is prohibited. No part of this book may be reproduced or transmitted in any form or by any means, electronic or mechanical, including photocopying, recording, or by any information storage and retrieval system without express written permission from the author / publisher.

ISBN-10:0615924204
ISBN-13:978-0-615-92420-5

Disclaimer: This book is designed to provide information and motivation to our readers. It is sold with the understanding that the publisher is not engaged to render any type of psychological, legal, or any other kind of professional advice. No warranties or guarantees are expressed or implied by the author, since every man has his own measure of faith. The individual author(s) shall not be liable for any physical, psychological, emotional, financial, or commercial damages, including; but not limited to, special, incidental, consequential or other damages. Our views and rights are the same: You are responsible for your own choices, actions, and results.

Dedication

This book is dedicated to my beautiful wife of more than twenty-six years, Mrs. Connie Mayo.

Thank you for being a crown to me, and I look forward to sharing many more loving years with you.

                Your Husband,
                Ronald

Introduction

I found my wife, Connie Germaine White, on April 8, 1985 at Marine Corp Air Station, Cherry Point, North Carolina. I met her at the base bowling alley. As we talked, I discovered that our likes and dislikes were the same; we were the same age, and we were born in the same month and year, only 17 days apart. We were both Christians raised in the church, so I thought I had all I needed to know.

The Proposal: Being in the military, I had just returned from a 45-day exercise at sea. I was scheduled to depart again in less than three weeks, and I would be gone for six to nine months. I'd already purchased a diamond engagement ring for her, so I took her to dinner. I arranged to have our waiter to bring the engagement ring with the desert. When dessert came, she opened the box, and I asked her to marry me. I vowed to take care of her for the rest of our lives. She cried and said, "Yes." Neither of us understood what we'd just agreed to, but with GOD, we have managed to stay married for over twenty-five years now.

Over the course of my marriage, I had to learn so much about my wife to remain married and to minimize conflict in our home. Over the course of my ministry, I have had to learn so much about women to help the men of GOD to remain married and to minimize conflict in their homes. This book is a compilation of what I have learned.

There are so many layers to women, and every married man, or man who desires to be married, one day needs to know them. If you are a married man, you've probably heard your wife say that you need to study her, and now you can. A Husband's Guide to Staying Married is a thought-provoking guide for husbands who want to understand their wives. There is much to be known about women, their choices and what they expect in the marriage setting. What you learn will amaze and relax you. You will also learn about your role as a husband and how you can better fill it. With divorce rates for believers spiraling out of control, there is a need for information, and lots of it. Believers need to learn how to stay married.

A Husband's Guide to Staying Married is a study guide for men who want to better understand their wives and learn how to build drama-free lives with them. In this book, you will learn what to expect over the course of your marriage and how to respond to the challenges that threaten the existence of your marriage. You will learn how to master your role as a husband through the Word of GOD. You will learn to see your wife past her imperfections as she does the same for you.

In A Husband's Guide to Staying Married, you will find scientific research that only confirms what GOD has already said. In this book, we will cover a variety of marriage-related topics that include, but are not limited to:

- Understanding the purpose of marriage.
- Better understanding yourself as a husband.
- Better understanding your wife.
- Resolving marriage conflict.

- Changing the course of your marriage.
- Overcoming adulterous mindsets.
- And much more.

This marriage guide will make a difference in your marriage. It is filled with information that you need and information that you want.

Table of Contents

Dedication..V
Introduction..VII
   The Purpose of Marriage...................................1
   Who Am I..13
   Who Is She..21
   As a Man Thinketh..29
   As a Woman Thinketh......................................43
   Studying Your Wife..61
   The Tests of Marriage.......................................73
   He Say, She Say...85
   Sowing Seeds In Your Marriage.......................97
   Understanding Your Wife................................111
   Accept It: She's Right Sometimes..................129
   Agreeing to Disagree.....................................135
   When Divorce Looks Better Than Your Wife..143
   Fruit of the Spirit Versus Fruit of the Flesh.....157
   Divorcing Yourself to Marry Her.....................169
   Training Your Mind to Forgive........................175
   Changing the Atmosphere In Your Marriage..189
   Changing the Blueprint of Your Marriage.......201
   Making the Best of What You Have...............219
   Adultery Stats and Revelations......................231
   Staying Together to Tell the Story..................247
   Scriptures Referencing Marriage...................267

The Purpose of Marriage

Most people want to be married; that goes without saying. One of the reasons that divorce is so prevalent today is the average believer thinks that marriage is just a union of the flesh. They believe that marriage is just two people coming together and committing to spend the rest of their lives with one another, but marriage goes so much deeper than that.

Everything in the earth, from the smallest to the greatest, has purpose. Every molecule of dirt was created by GOD and is known by GOD. Every inch of rain was created by GOD and is counted by GOD. Even the hairs on your head are counted. So what then is the purpose of marriage? To get a better look at marriage, we must first examine GOD'S relationship with man. Genesis 1:27 reads, *"So God created man in his own image, in the image of God created he him; male and female created he them."* Why did GOD create man? To fill the earth, of course. Why did GOD create man in HIS own likeness? Because man was made by GOD for GOD. GOD is Supreme; HE is Creator of all things; Heaven and Earth. HE is ruler of the universe. When GOD created man, HE gave man dominion over the earth and everything in it. HE made man like HIM. As a matter of fact, the Bible refers to us as "gods." Recall what JESUS said to the Jews who accused HIM of blasphemy. *"Jesus answered them, "Jesus answered them, Is it not written in your law, I said, Ye are gods? If he called them gods, unto whom the word of God came, and the scripture cannot be broken; Say ye of him, whom the Father hath sanctified, and sent into the world, Thou blasphemest; because I said, I am the Son of God? If I do not the works of my Father, believe me not. But if I do, though ye believe not me, believe the works: that ye may know, and believe, that the Father is in me, and I in him" (John 10:34-38).* GOD created us

The Purpose of Marriage

like HIM because HE created us to act like HIM. HE made us a little lower than angels, and HE created us for HIMSELF. We were created to worship HIM and subdue the earth.

Why did GOD create woman? Genesis 2:18 reads, *"And the LORD God said, It is not good that the man should be alone; I will make him an help meet for him."* Woman was created to be a help meet for man. A wife was created to accompany her husband in purpose with GOD. She was created to love and be loved. Just as GOD provides for us, a husband is the provider for his home. A husband should have the very nature of GOD. He is a covering, a protector, a friend and a lover. Just as man was created a little lower than angels, woman was created a little lower than man. This does not mean that she is not equally as important as the man. After all, we were created a little lower than angels; nevertheless, we are just as loved as the angels of GOD. Angels are higher because angels are GOD'S firstborn children. Man is a little lower than angels because man came after angels, and woman is a little lower than man because woman came after the man and

The Purpose of Marriage

from the man. *"And the LORD God caused a deep sleep to fall upon Adam, and he slept: and he took one of his ribs, and closed up the flesh instead thereof; And the rib, which the LORD God had taken from man, made he a woman, and brought her unto the man. And Adam said, This is now bone of my bones, and flesh of my flesh: she shall be called Woman, because she was taken out of Man" (Genesis 1:21-23).*

So what then is the purpose of marriage? Marriage is relationship; it is very similar to our relationships with GOD, and it teaches us the importance of the order of GOD. Before sin visited mankind, this order was not enforced because it did not have to be enforced, but once mankind fell, GOD had to enforce the order to keep mankind from falling. Man was called the head of the woman because man was created by GOD before the woman, and woman was created by GOD for the man. Because of this, women are weaker than men. 1 Peter 3:7 confirms this. *"Likewise, ye husbands, dwell with them according to*

The Purpose of Marriage

knowledge, giving honour unto the wife, as unto the weaker vessel, and as being heirs together of the grace of life; that your prayers be not hindered."

Marriage is purposed in relationship. GOD created us to have a relationship with HIM, and HE created the union of marriage so that man could have a direct relationship with another person in the earth. But why didn't GOD create another man for Adam? It's simple. For the very reason that HE is the only GOD and there is no other GOD but HIM. Adam was a "god" in the realm of the earth. He was given dominion over the earth; therefore, the earth didn't need another "god". Instead, GOD created a help meet for Adam just as HE created Adam as a help meet for HIMSELF.

The purpose of man is to fill and subdue the earth. The purpose of the husband is to cover, protect and provide for his wife, and to raise up children after his own heart with her. The purpose of the wife is to be a help meet to her

The Purpose of Marriage

husband. She is the womb-man or woman; she is a giver of life, a living vessel.

When GOD called man the head of the woman, HE did not mean that women were not as important to HIM as men were. The order of GOD is the protection of GOD. GOD understands how we were created; after all, HE is our Creator. HE understands how the enemy works. Satan goes after the weaker vessel. That's why he went after Eve in the Garden of Eden. Satan did not go after Adam because Adam was the stronger of the two. So GOD placed woman under the head or authority of the man for her protection. This was not done to minimize who the woman was or her relationship with GOD. It was to keep the enemy from deceiving her again and again. The husband is the head of the wife, just as CHRIST is the head of the husband. Many people don't contend with the fact that as men, we are in subjection to CHRIST, but there is a lot of resistance about the woman being in subjection to the man. This is oftentimes because man is imperfect, and many women have subjected themselves to ungodly men, and these ungodly men did ungodly things to them. Nevertheless, the role of the husband can never be truly diminished. Without JESUS as his head, a man would be in subjection to his flesh. His flesh would lead him, and the flesh is oftentimes led by the enemy because the lustful desires of the flesh lead to death. Therefore, any man not led by CHRIST could not make a proper head. At the same time, when a woman becomes the wife of a man, she has to follow the order of GOD to remain under the protection of GOD. She is the help meet of her husband, but a GOD-fearing husband would not abuse his authority, just as CHRIST did not abuse HIS authority. Instead, a Godly man will glorify GOD through every avenue, including his relationship with his wife.

Marriage also weakens the enemy when both parties involved stand with GOD against the enemy. When we stand with GOD, we will automatically stand together as a couple, because we will be one with GOD'S plan for us and GOD'S plan for the earth. But when our flesh takes the lead, we become individually-minded to the point where we stand for ourselves and against our spouses. There are several reasons that the enemy tries to divide a marriage. Here are a few scriptures to give you a little more insight:

- **Matthew 18:20- "For where two or three are gathered together in my name, there am I in the midst of them."** Satan knows that he cannot successfully oppose a team, but he can oppose an individual. Therefore, the enemy's strategy is to divide and conquer. That's why he went after Eve individually in the Garden of Eden. He didn't tempt Adam and Eve as one person; he tempted Eve because he knew that Eve would follow up by tempting Adam.

- **Ecclesiastes 4:12- "And if one prevail against him, two shall withstand him; and a threefold cord is not quickly broken."** As written, one can prevail against the enemy, but two will withstand him. What does it mean to "withstand" him? Google defines the word "withstand" as: *remain undamaged or unaffected by; resist.* Therefore, when two stand up against the enemy, they will resist him; they won't be damaged by him and they won't be affected by his darts. If the couple stands together in CHRIST against the enemy, GOD will stand in as the third fold in their cord.

- **Mark 10:27- "And Jesus looking upon them saith, With men it is impossible, but not with God: for with God all things are possible."** With GOD, there is order. When you follow the order, nothing will be impossible for you. Unity simply gives you too much power against the enemy, and he doesn't want anyone to have that kind of power.

- **Proverbs 18:22- "Whoso findeth a wife findeth a good thing, and obtaineth favour of the LORD."** One of the words that is an opposite of the word "favor" is "hindrance." If GOD favors a man for finding a wife, just how much more will a man be hindered who mistreats his wife? 1 Peter 3:7 reads, *"Likewise, you husbands, dwell with them according to knowledge, giving honor unto the wife, as unto the weaker vessel, and as being heirs together of the grace of life; **that your prayers be not hindered.**"* Google defines "hindrance" as: *a thing that provides resistance, delay, or obstruction to something or someone.* Anytime a man dishonors his wife and allows strife to reside in his home, GOD will resist him; his promotion will be delayed, and his prayers will be blocked. After all, the word "obstruction" is defined by Google as: *block (an opening, path, road, etc.); be or get in the way of.*

As you can see, the enemy's plan is to simply stand between us and GOD because Satan desires to be our god. He is jealous of GOD, and anything that empowers you is a threat to him. GOD-ordained marriages threaten the enemy. In addition, with a help meet, a man can become a better man when he learns to

The Purpose of Marriage

love and appreciate the woman sent to help him. Marriage teaches us about our strengths, our weaknesses and shows us every area in our lives that needs improvement. Marriage causes us to go before the throne of GOD seeking deliverance from mindsets that threaten our relationships with our spouses, for it is those very mindsets that threaten our relationship with our GOD. Iniquity hides itself deep within a man's heart, but GOD hands each spouse the key to the heart of their other half. For this reason, a wife can pull out of a man what no mother, father, sister or brother could have ever pulled out of him. If iniquity is hidden in a man, the wife will find it, expose it and yell at it. As men of GOD, it is our duty to then take what was discovered before the LORD. This is to say that a help meet helps you to become a better you if you only let her operate in her role as a wife, even when she does not operate the way you want her to operate. After all, it isn't the clockwise motion that releases a thing; it is often the counterclockwise motion coupled with strength that provides the resistance necessary to release whatever has been held up. Whatever stands in your heart as a strongman will be challenge by your GOD-ordained wife, because she has direct access to your heart. She's not opposing you when she exposes your hidden sin; instead, she is acting as a help meet.

GOD'S reason for instituting the marriage arrangement is to give you a better look at HIS relationship with you. You will better understand how HE feels when your spouse makes you feel the same way. You will learn to change your ways towards HIM when you learn to change your ways toward your spouse. Our relationships with our spouses work simultaneously with our relationships with GOD. When we learn to be better sons, we learn to be better husbands, and when we learn to be better husbands, we learn to be better sons.

Who Am I

One of the contributing factors to a bad marriage is lack of knowledge. In addition to knowing and accepting JESUS CHRIST as your LORD and Savior, you have to know and accept who you are as a person. The average man does not know his own identity. Instead, he has come to identify himself by the face he sees in the mirror and what others have said of him. If he's funny, he knows he's funny. If he's mean, he know he's mean. Whatever a man is on the exterior is known of him, but who a man is on the inside is rarely known.

You'll come across a lot of men who will tell you about strength they didn't know they possessed until they had no choice but to use it. You'll come across men who didn't know how compassionate they were until they saw another human being who needed a warm embrace. At the same time, you will meet men who didn't know how evil they were until they were given the opportunity to show the content of their wicked hearts. Oftentimes, these characters marry with a misconception of who they are; therefore, they meet and marry women who fit their mental mold of themselves. Their marriages fail because their true identities keep being revealed to themselves and their wives, but because of lack of knowledge, they don't recognize that their behaviors and thoughts are evidence of the fruit they bear. Instead, they blame their wives for their hang ups. A man who does not know his own identity may say things like:

- "She brings out the worst in me. I don't normally act like that, but she knows where my triggers are."
- "She made me hit her."
- "It's her fault. Everything was going fine until she opened her mouth."

What that man is really saying is he is coming to find out who he is every time adversity steps on his toes. That's why a man should never marry a woman until he knows how he'll respond to fear, rejection or negative words. He needs to know how he fights. He needs to know if he'd be willing to hit a woman, for example, so he can seek deliverance. Sadly enough, many men think that their identities are wrapped up in their wives. If you don't know who you are before you meet and marry your wife, you may lose her when who you truly are grows up and is revealed.

Just who are you? The answer is wrapped up and packaged in the heart of GOD. It is deep within the chambers of obedience and in the vein of truth. You have to get to know the depths of who GOD is before you will be granted access to the knowledge of who you are. That's because a man who uncovers his own identity without first discovering who GOD is may end up worshipping himself and placing himself on a pedestal. It goes without saying that his haughty look would cause him to be knocked off his pedestal by the truth, and destruction will overtake him. There is so much wrapped up in your identity, such as healing, prosperity and a sound mind. These aren't just added blessings that we can afford when we serve and believe GOD; healing, prosperity and sane are who we are. We simply lose our identities in sin, and obedience helps us to get back to who we are.

Knowing who you are will help you to marry the right wife. For example, a man may join a motorcycle gang and develop an identity from within that gang. He gets tattooed up and gets a biker babe to complete his persona. At that moment in his life, she may be the best girlfriend he has ever had because she fits so well into who he is today. Just imagine that he married that woman, and he eventually got saved, but she did not. She loves the wild life, and he loves the LORD. He will likely lose his wife because they are now unequally yoked. His old character married her, but when his real character emerged, she wasn't attracted to him. Sometimes, the story isn't as dramatic as that, but the endings are the same.

Who Am I

There is no place to find your identity except in obeying GOD and doing what HE called you to do. We look for clues of who we are in our conversations and in other people's personal opinions. That's why we oftentimes find it funny when someone reveals something to us about ourselves that we were unaware of. We want to get to know ourselves better, but the truth is hidden in GOD. That's why GOD told us to seek HIM and HIS will first before anything or anyone else. *"But seek ye first the kingdom of God, and his righteousness; and all these things shall be added unto you"* (Matthew 6:33).

Any time a man does not know who he is, he will likely meet and marry a woman who does not know who she is. When they come together, they start a war on words, trying to uncover what they believe to be one another's flaws. They then start a series of behaviors designed to get their new partners to become what they need at that stage in their lives. This is undoubtedly like taking directions from the devil, because a lost person is handing another lost soul a map to nowhere. When the relationships end, each party has to find their way back to what they once knew of themselves to start their journeys all over again.

Your success is tied up in your true identity. You can never properly provide for a wife when you are unsure of yourself. Sure, you can end up with a decent job, but you'll become dependent on that job for your identity and your lifestyle, and this is a form of idolatry. GOD wants you to depend on HIM, and HE wants you to live a life pleasing to HIM. HE wants to reveal secrets to you of your inner man. HE wants to break that old man off you so that who you are can stand up renewed, but this takes a process that many are fearful of entering or too weak to endure. Make no mistake about it; there is no getting around this process. Most people don't submit to this process until they've gotten older and realized that this process is necessary for longevity, peace and successful marriages.

Who Am I

Just ask GOD to reveal your true identity to you. Also, prepare to enter the process where your identity will be caused to come to the forefront and reveal itself to you. Don't give up while going through this process. Instead, embrace it and trust GOD with your soul. When you discover who you are, the next stop will be to pick up your wife so she can accompany you in purpose. There are no detours in life. We can only ask GOD for HIS will to be done, and we have to submit to HIS will for our lives. We often make things more complicated than they are. Remember, just ask HIM, and HE will tell you.

Who Is She

Who is this woman that I've married? At some point, every married man has to face this question in relation to their wives. We meet and marry the women who seemed to fit so perfectly into our lives. In the first few months following the marriage, we begin to find clues that the women we chose to marry are not who we thought they were, and this isn't always a bad thing. It's scary, but not bad.

GOD locked up the truth inside of HIM, and HE gave us the keys to access this truth through JESUS CHRIST. We simply have to ask for it and believe GOD for it, but oftentimes, we are afraid of the unmasked truth. After all, we fell in love with our own ideas of who our wives were, and we don't want anything (including the truth) to come in and show us a different picture of our wives. How could we handle that? After all, we'd then have to get to know the real her better and then hope that we'll like her. But the fact is we do not know the wholeness of who our wives are. We only know what they have shown us and some of what GOD has shown them; therefore, we have to get to know them better over the years. As the years pass us by, we find out so many fascinating things about our wives, and we also discover so many interesting facts about ourselves. Some of what we discover about our wives aren't welcomed revelations. As a matter of fact, some of what we are forced to confront tests the very limitations of our understandings. That's because we have this preconceived idea of what a wife does and what a wife is not supposed to do. Any time our wives test those limits, we have to be reeled back in by knowledge before we can start our healing processes in understanding. Every time we learn something new about our wives, we have to get to know that part of her better, whether we want to or not. If what we find out is bad, we have to speak with them about what we've realized, pray for them and cover them so those ways can be put to rest. At the same time, our wives' ways help to uncover our hidden ways. Anytime we discover something negative about ourselves, we should ask the LORD to turn that thing into a positive, because these ways and mindsets can't come along with us on our marriage journeys.

As husbands, we are imparters. We impart who we are into our wives, and they become one with us. Pay attention to a woman who has been married more than one time. She's a different woman for every man that she's married, because she had to learn how to be each man's wife. You may find a woman who was very quiet and reserved in her first marriage suddenly become flamboyant in her second marriage. She's a help meet, and she will naturally fit the need of her husband, and she will pick up on who he is. What does this mean to us? It means that our wives are amazing vessels who carry not only their own personalities, but they are made to carry ours as well. At the same time, no woman knows the entirety of who she is. This is revealed to her over time and throughout her faith walk in CHRIST. This is also revealed to her through the trials and tribulations she faces.

As her identity is revealed to her, you will find that there are days when she's pleasant to live with, and then there are those days when she is not pleasant to live with. There are those times when she is transitioning into who she is, and there are those times when she has fallen back into who she was. As husbands, we have to encourage their continued growths, and we have to continue to search out their hearts for them.

Before we met our wives, GOD placed us on a journey towards our wives. On this path, a lot of what was in us was challenged and terminated from our lives. We experienced the highs and lows of living, but more than that, we learned how to roll with the punches. One day, our season to find our wives was upon us, and

Who is She

GOD gave us the key to finding them. But here's a little known fact: When you find your wife, you have to continue to find her every day, even after the marriage. How is that? There are so many levels to who your wife is, and these revelations of her have not yet come forth to meet the world. Her whole identity is locked up in CHRIST, and we have to continue to search the heart of CHRIST to get the pieces of who she is. Eventually, we'll have enough pieces to put together the big picture, but searching her out keeps the marriage interesting and fun. A man who does not seek to know his wife better is a man who has robbed himself, his wife and the world of an opportunity to get to know a pretty amazing individual.

The average man gets to know the obvious things about his wife. He knows her favorite colors; he knows her shoe size, and what foods she is allergic to. He knows her relationship boundaries, and he knows what she believes about GOD. Nevertheless, the average man stops right there and stays put with who she projects and believes herself to be rather than seeking GOD to get a better view of his wife. After all, revealing who she is will help to review who we are as men. Of course, this requires work, love, faith, courage and perseverance. Our wives are our faith tests, and our ribs. They were pulled out of us, and now we have to pull who they are out of them.

You can't be happily married if you don't search the heart of your wife for the hidden woman, because at any given moment, your wife will need answers when she is in transition. Our transitional stages are the stages where we experience fear, anxiety and birthing pains. It's like going through deliverance, only your wife will be delivered from who she is to arrive in who she is to be. During these transitional periods, you have to continually make sure that your wife is covered, encouraged and reassured. At the same time, you can't allow the enemy to weigh you down with the fears of who she is becoming. There are many guys out there who will happily pull the plug on their

Who is She

wives' transitions because of fear. What they end up with are unhappy and confused wives who are out of the will of GOD.

Continue to search for the hidden chambers of your wife's heart. In doing so, she may resist you, she may question you, but she will also appreciate and love you for wanting to get to know her even more. You'll watch your wife grow as she makes her life's rounds throughout each day. You'll see her encourage others, and she will be a living testimony without opening her mouth, because other women will see how you treat your wife. When they see her being treated like a woman of GOD should be treated, many of them will wait for their GOD-ordained husbands instead of dating every Jack, Tom, Tyrone and John that flirts with them. Your marriage should be ministry, and your marriage should reflect your love of GOD. Search for your wife inside of your wife. No, the person won't change. Like fine wine, she'll just get better and better with age.

As a Man Thinketh

Everything in the earth started off as a seed, and every seed must complete a cycle of life. Once a seed has transitioned from being a seed into adulthood, that seed must then release seeds after its own kind. An orange tree can only bear oranges, and oranges can only bear orange seeds. If those seeds take root, they will eventually become orange trees graced by seed-bearing oranges, and the cycle will continue.

Just as an orange seed gives birth to an orange tree, everything that is alive will eventually give birth to something after its own kind. This is because GOD is a life-giver. HE breathed the breath of life into man, and man became a living soul. (See Genesis 2:7). HE made man in HIS image; therefore, man is created to be like his Creator. A man bears fruit, and his seed will always reflect what type of tree he is.

When a man becomes an adult, he searches for his identity through friendships, relationships, career choices and so on. This is the time when he is searching for his fruit. Every man must know what type of tree he is before he can start the process of budding into who he really is. During this search, he will oftentimes find clues as to who he is, but never the entire picture of who he will become. If he's diligent, he will learn that he's diligent; if he is short-tempered, life will teach him this, and if he is patient, time will reflect this. These clues not only develop him as a man, but they begin the developmental process of him as a husband. That's why it is very important that a man go through his seasons of change before he is entrusted to carry on the role of a husband; otherwise, he will search for his identity in the midst of his marriage. When a man doesn't know his identity before he enters the state of marriage, he will likely exit the marriage because the woman he married was a perfect match for who he thought he was. As he discovers his identity, he will find out that the wife he chose for himself is not a match for the man that he is; she is a better match for the boy that he was.

Nevertheless, in CHRIST, we are all called to transition, but during this transition, we cannot walk away from the seeds we have sown. Instead, we are now responsible for helping them to transition. Therefore, when a man discovers who he is in CHRIST and has entered maturity, he cannot walk away from the wife that he chose in his youth. Instead, he must continue to lead and cover her; he must continue to love and nourish her, for she is a seed as well. That's why GOD gave a commandment to the husband. Proverbs 5:18 reads, *"Let your fountain be blessed: and rejoice with the wife of your youth."*

There is a reason that GOD told a man to

rejoice with the wife of his youth. GOD is the Creator of man; therefore, he knows how a man's mind transitions as he develops. HE knows those pivotal points in a man's life that steers him toward the wrong choices. HE knows that as a man thinks, so is he. In other words, if a man develops a wrong way of thinking, he will develop a wrong way of living. He will become the very way he thinks. If a man develops a wrong way of thinking, he will not honor his wife because to him, who she is does not fit with who he is becoming. In doing so, he will dishonor GOD by dishonoring her. For this reason, GOD warned the husbands in 1 Peter 3:7 by saying, *"Likewise, ye husbands, dwell with them according to knowledge, giving honour unto the wife, as unto the weaker vessel, and as being heirs together of the grace of life; that your prayers be not hindered."*

If a man allows himself to "fall out of love" with his wife, he will not only start a cycle of bad seeds in his life, but he will set in motion a lesson for his children that is almost surely to be repeated. His choices as a husband will not only affect him, but his choices will affect everyone in his household, because he is called to lead the house. A man is the head of his house, and as the head, any choices he makes will affect everyone he is supposed to be covering. If he dishonors his wife, his daughters will allow themselves to be dishonored, disrespected and distrusting of men. His sons will oftentimes follow in his footsteps, abandoning the wives of their youth to embrace every stage of development that they enter.

In life, we all go through stages of development, and every stage that we enter marks a new way of thinking for us. Suddenly, yesterday's way of thinking won't be so entertaining today. This means that even the people we invited into our lives in the past won't be so welcomed by us in our futures. This includes that spouse that we chose for ourselves during the highlights of our youthfulness. When the wife doesn't transition along with the husband, as men, we will find ourselves inwardly seeking a woman after our own hearts. We may not speak this openly, but secretly, that hunger is there. When this hunger comes upon a man, his mind starts to shift towards getting that hunger filled. Even if he does not start an adulterous affair outwardly, he may begin one inwardly. For this reason, GOD warned us about even the way that we think. *"But I say unto you, That whosoever looks on a woman to lust after her has committed adultery with her already in his heart" (Matthew 5:28).* In this scripture, GOD is warning the husbands to beware of their thinking processes. HE is warning husbands to grab the wheels of their thought processes and steer them back into loving their wives, even when those wheels are hard to turn.

But what is a wife to a man? Why is she so important to GOD? Why does GOD protect her from the unmerciful acts of a bored man? A wife is a helpmate to her spouse. More than that, a wife will birth sons and daughters who will follow after their parents' lead. A wife is the weaker vessel; a creature who GOD carefully handed to the husband HE'D chosen for her. She is a treasure who is so valued by GOD that she had to be hidden in HIM. She is a fragile creation only to be held by the man who GOD has revealed her value to. When GOD uncovers this secret as to who she is, and the hidden treasures of her heart, HE expects the man HE has blessed to have her to continue to cover and shield her. When GOD blesses a husband with his wife, GOD gives him more than just a wife; GOD gives him favor. *"Whosoever finds a wife finds a good thing, and obtains favor of the LORD" (Proverbs 18:22).*

The way a man thinks will affect every aspect of his life. It will affect how he fathers his children; it will affect how he leads his home, and it will affect his very relationship with GOD. As with all things in life, a man's mind will change as the seasons play out in his life. Most men get wiser as they get older, and then there are the ones who don't transition into wise men. Instead, they just transition into what many refer to as "old fools". During each developmental marker in a man's life, he is expected to check in with GOD and learn to fly in his new mentality. This isn't always easy, especially when change comes upon a man suddenly and he doesn't understand it. A large number of men see this change as a threat to the identities they have grown accustomed to; therefore, they oppose this change by acting out. For example, there is a period in a man's life that many refer to as a midlife crisis. During this time, the reality of growing old is challenging a man's fantasy of remaining young. In his attempt to stand up against Mother Nature, he may go out and buy a motorcycle or a convertible, or he may take up some youthful activity. While in a midlife crisis, many husbands leave their wives for younger women, hoping to win the battle against aging. Of course, this doesn't work, and reality hits these men where it hurts them the most.

The wife, on the other hand, is still a fruit-bearing tree that will continue to develop over the course of her life. It goes without saying that when a man transitions into a new way of thinking, as the leader, he is supposed to help usher his wife into this new mindset. Nevertheless, many husbands find themselves abandoning their posts as husbands to chase after illusions of finding women who they believe are already in line with their way of thinking. This is a mistake for so many reasons. Here are some facts to consider:

1. Would you build a house and abandon it to start building where someone else has left off? In doing so, many husbands have found out the hard way that another man's establishment was custom created by that man, for that man and could never be inhabited comfortably by another man.

2. A man cannot appreciate what he did not build. What this means is a man can always look in awe at the beauty of another establishment, but he could never appreciate it or know its real value if he did not invest in it. Nevertheless, even when a man does not consciously appreciate his wife, subconsciously, he knows that she is an invaluable treasure

that can never be replaced.

3. Any opportunity to build on another establishment outside of your covenant of marriage is not built on a godly foundation; therefore, its doomsday begins counting down the day it takes form.

4. Any time life offers a man the opportunity to trade in something valuable in his life, it's a test that tries him to see if he is mature enough to enter a new stage of life; one where he could enjoy the fruits of his decisions. Ironically, life never offers you a valuable trade-in. Instead, we are offered new and beautiful junk as trade-ins for our familiar and invaluable treasures that have withstood the tests of time. It's simply not worth it.

5. Many men don't realize that just as they have been building their marriages with their wives, their wives have been crucial to their development as well. The man is a builder, but a wife will take

what a man builds, decorate it and make it a home.

What should a man do when he begins to transition and does not like how his wife is fitting into his life? It's simple: He is to cover, protect, lead, teach, exalt, exhort and reprove her. This is a very important time in his relationship with his wife, and it is a golden opportunity for him to prove himself worthy of being called a husband. This is a time where he can show GOD that HIS favor is well-deserved and appreciated. During his time of transition, he can show his sons how to lead their homes from one blessing into the next, and he can show his daughters the characteristics of godly men, so they won't fall into the arms of the ungodly. During a transition, a husband has the opportunity to show himself worthy of receiving a promotion by GOD. This is a time when he can enter a peaceful rest with the wife of his youth and enjoy what he has built for himself and his family. *"His lord said unto him, Well done, good and faithful servant; thou hast been faithful over a few things, I will make thee ruler over many things: enter thou into the joy of thy lord" (Matthew 25:23).*

You will notice that in a large number of divorces, the couple cites their reason for divorce as, "We grew apart. We weren't seeing eye-to-eye." What they are really saying is they entered transition individually and not as one person as GOD has called them to be. They entered transition as a house divided, and because of this, their marriage did not stand. Transition is like an earthquake: either you will grab, protect and cover one another, or you will try to save yourself, even if it means the other person must be sacrificed. Anytime the cursed word of "me" enters a marriage, the blessed "we" will be sacrificed. The word "me" divides marriages down the middle and opens up the home to devils. In unity, however, the enemy has no place. *"And if one prevail against him, two shall withstand him; and a threefold cord is not quickly broken" (Ecclesiastes 4:12).*

The correct way to transition is to stay in the will of GOD and ask GOD to carry you through the turbulence of change. During transition, you will have many questions, but GOD wants you to ask HIM for whatever you need. *"Ye lust, and have not: ye kill, and desire to have, and cannot obtain: ye fight and war, yet ye have not, because ye ask not" (James 4:2).* During transition, many negative feelings may try to embrace you, but you must reject them to accept GOD'S new assignment for you. Transition is never easy. It's confusing, challenging and sometimes depressing; nevertheless, it is necessary. Every change a man endures amplifies that man's strength, character and endurance, and builds him up until he becomes like the tower of Babel. His understanding will reach up into Heaven, but his words will be clear wisdom that any man or woman can understand because he didn't build himself up on the wrong things; instead, he let GOD build him. During transition, a man will reach the heights of new understanding and the breadths of knowledge. Like a good husband, he will move his family from one way of thinking into another. His marriage will stand the tests of time because he will withstand the tests of the enemy. Instead of allowing himself to fear tomorrow, he will learn to overcome today until tomorrow becomes another day he has defeated.

As a Woman Thinketh

It goes without saying that men and women see life from different angles. For men, life is simple; all you have to do is live it. For women, life is a little more complicated and more hands-on. Because of this difference in our ways of thinking, women often find themselves wanting to "work things out", whereas men like to sit on the sidelines and watch things play out on their own. A man only wants to tackle whatever situation he believes he can bring down easily, but if a problem looks to be a giant to him, he prefers to move over and let that giant pass him by. A woman, on the other hand, wants that giant to be overcome because she fears that the giant will return and terrorize the marriage again and again until it has been defeated or until the marriage has succumbed to the strength of the strongman.

As a Woman Thinketh

Trying to find a bridge of understanding between women and men has proved to be difficult but not impossible. This meeting ground is attainable only when both parties agree with GOD.

Women are fascinating characters because they are one of the greatest mysteries in the earth. Their patterns of thinking are so complex that no scientist, doctor or psychologist has ever been able to scale their minds or breech their understandings. Nevertheless, in their complexity, they aren't impossible to understand; you simply need GOD to open up the door of understanding before you can reach the whole heart of a woman. This sacred door is guarded and can only be entered by the man to whom GOD has given the key. Any man who illegally takes a woman and makes her his wife will suffer the roarings of a misunderstood woman whose demands to be understood appear to be out of his reach and beyond his understanding. Any man who illegally takes a woman to be his wife will eventually call her a "nag" after he has searched for answers as to what she wants and has no success in obtaining those answers.

Just as a man thinks, so he is; as a woman thinks, so is she. This is why a husband has to be absolutely careful what he causes his wife to believe. Whatever she believes will manifest as a part of her; therefore, a woman has to believe that she is appreciated. She has to know and believe that she is beautiful, invaluable and needed. In believing this, a woman will continue to blossom because women are hands-on creatures. Because they are hands-on, any giant that passes by a woman will be attacked by the woman it is attempting to terrorize. Pay attention to a lioness. The male lions in a pride aren't the most aggressive of the gender parties. Instead, most outside males who attempt to enter that pride's territory are attacked by the females of that territory, not the males. Male lions do attack other male lions who encroach upon their territory, but this is mostly done when there are no females around or when a female lion shows distress at the presence of another male. This is to say that women are territorial creatures who do not like problems entering the borders of their marriages or territories. This is why you will find that a wife will go on and on about a problem in the marriage until that problem has been removed. It's not that she wants to war with her husband; the issue is often that she wants her husband to war with the problem. If he doesn't tackle the issue, the wife will attempt to tackle it herself, and she may be overcome by the issue if it is too big for her.

It goes without saying that every woman is different, just as every man is different. Every woman has a mindset that even she has trouble understanding. That's why you will find that women will go on and on about an issue in the marriage, but you can always confuse them with one question. Any time a wife is upset and being argumentative, the best question to ask her is: "Without all of the talking, be direct and tell me what the problem is, as well as how you think we should fix it." Such questioning can be complex to a woman who recognizes that a giant is present but has not put too much thought into how that giant is to be handled. That's because women don't care how a man fights a giant, as long as he makes that giant disappear.

Just as men develop and mature into new ways of thinking, women develop and mature into new ways of thinking. When a woman outgrows a man and arrives at maturity faster than he does, she may become more and more argumentative because of fear. A new way of thinking is like a new and unexplored territory, and women like to be accompanied by their husbands when they arrive in these foreign places. Without their mates, they feel exposed, unprotected and lonely. A woman can physically have her husband near her and still feel alone when she has matured into a new way of thinking that the husband has not yet arrived at. This is because a wife is her husband's helpmate, but she cannot help him on an assignment that he has not yet shown up for.

When a wife matures faster than her husband, she will oftentimes have trouble submitting to him as GOD has commanded her to do. You'll notice in the scriptures that GOD commanded man to love his wife, but HE commanded wives to submit to their husbands. Why is this? It's simple: A wife is designed in love and will continue to love her husband throughout the tests of time. Men, on the other hand, can enter relationships physically without entering them emotionally. Because many women transition into maturity faster than their counterparts, women had to be commanded to submit to their husbands. This commandment was given to keep women from losing respect for their husbands, and to keep a woman from becoming high-minded or prideful. After all, as she thinks, so she will be. This means that a woman who does not honor her husband, but continues to belittle him as she transitions, can slow down or terminate the development of her husband. At the same time, a wife who submits to her husband, loves her husband, and remains chaste, will cause her husband to seek new knowledge so that he can relate to her and properly cover her.

In the cycle of life, women are believed to develop into maturity faster than men. The truth is, women don't develop faster; they simply embrace change faster than men. Men are oftentimes intimidated by change and will evade it at all costs. Women are curious creatures who see change as giant steps towards their dreams. Like a tree, a woman can grow to be a fruitful blessing that keeps on giving when properly cared for. Women are not only fertile physically, but women are spiritually fertile. This means that whatever seed a man sows into his wife will grow up as his wife. Women will take everything that is given to them and birth something from it. Again, if you have ever seen a woman who has been twice married, you will notice that she is not the same type of wife with one man as she was with the other. That's because a woman will continue to birth out whatever a man sows into her. If you sow love in her, she will give you a greater love in return. If you sow respect in her, she will respect you that much more in return. At the same time, if you sow contention in her, she will be even more contentious than you are because a wife will take the seed that her husband hands her and give him the fruit thereof.

How a woman thinks will affect her children, and it will affect how her husband relates to her. This is why it is important for a husband to take the time out to study the WORD with his wife and to communicate with his wife. In doing this, he helps to maintain a mutual understanding in the home, as opposed to getting a front row seat to Mark 3:25: *"And if a house be divided against itself, that house cannot stand."* Divides in a home aren't there because of contention, as many people believe. Divides come in when transition has embraced one spouse without embracing the other. Oftentimes, leaders try to help couples with whatever they are arguing about, when the real issue is the couple not knowing how to stay balanced while in transition.

Just what is a husband to a wife, and why is he so important to her? Why is his role so important to GOD? A husband is created in the image of GOD. He is a man who was granted the favor of being a husband. In his new role, he was handed something very valuable to GOD; something that would be invaluable to him, and that something is his wife. To a wife, the husband represents so many things. He carries in him revelations as to who she is, and he was given an assignment by GOD to carry out. His wife was given that same assignment, to come along as a helpmate, but this is the curb that loses so many people. When the Bible calls her a helpmate, it doesn't mean that she is his personal assistant to help him to embrace the pleasures of life. She is his helpmate to accompany him in righteousness and the works that GOD has assigned them to in the earth. Women are thinkers. That's why Proverbs 31:16 tells us, *"She considereth a field, and buyeth it: with the fruit of her hands she planteth a vineyard."* In this, the scriptures don't just say she buys a field. It tells us that she first considers the field. Because women spend so much time in their thoughts, they can be a treasure or a debt to the men that have them. Because women are thinkers, they are often faith-filled creatures who can usher change into their homes just by believing GOD for change. Consider what happened with the woman who had the issue of blood. She didn't just touch the hem of the LORD'S garment; the Bible tells us that she "thought" that she could be healed by touching the hem of the LORD'S garments. Therefore, the seed of faith had been sown, and she followed that seed up with the works.

Mark 5:25-34 reads:

"And a certain woman, who had an issue of blood twelve years,

And had suffered many things of many physicians, and had spent all that she had, and was no better, but rather grew worse,

When she had heard of Jesus, came in the crowd behind, and touched his garment.

For she said, If I may touch but his clothes, I shall be whole.

And immediately the fountain of her blood was dried up; and she felt in her body that she was

healed of that disease.
And Jesus, immediately knowing in himself that power had gone out of him, turned about in the crowd, and said, Who touched my clothes?
And his disciples said unto him, You see the multitude thronging you, and you say, Who touched me?
And he looked round about to see her that had done this thing.
But the woman fearing and trembling, knowing what was done in her, came and fell down before him, and told him all the truth.
*And he said unto her, Daughter, **your faith has made you whole**; go in peace, and be whole of your disease."*

This scripture is important for so many reasons, but one of those reasons is the statement that reads, *"Your faith has made you whole; go in peace."* What does this scripture tell us? When a woman's faith (what she believes) has been challenged, she will not be at peace. For this reason, it is very important for a man to maintain peace in his house through Bible studies and by respecting and loving his wife. A husband has to be very careful when sowing words into his wife, as those words will grow up and either develop or come against his wife's faith. If a woman believes her marriage is in danger, she will become a danger to her marriage; therefore, to maintain peace, a woman must maintain faith, and a man must remain faithful in delivering the WORD in his home.

Women transition differently than men do. While men often search for their identities outwardly and make their transitions silently, women often search for their identities inwardly and make their transitions publicly. For example, when a woman goes through transition, she will often question herself, her decisions and the people around her. Women don't often buy motorcycles or any other fast or flashy vehicles when they are confronted by change. Instead, many women will consider different areas to transition in. Some women may decide to go to church more; some may consider doing more in their communities, while others may decide to change their hair. What a woman searches for in transition will always depend on whatever void or need she feels she has. Publicly, many women will tell their friends about the changes they are going through.

Women think in patterns, and their thoughts are like the lasers of a gun. They will point their thoughts at a certain thing, person or situation, and it is hard to deflect their thoughts to anything else until that matter has been dealt with. When a woman's mind is pointed in a certain direction, she will talk for days, months and even years about whatever distraction has crossed her path. To remedy this, the man in her life must deal with the distraction in her life. He must take on any giant in her path, even if that giant seems too big for him. In doing so, he will repeatedly gain the respect of his wife, because women are attracted to warriors. As a warrior, a man doesn't always have to go into a physical war; he simply needs to war in the spirit and aggressively take on whatever giants are confronting his wife. Sometimes, this means he must directly address his wife and whatever mindsets she has submitted to.

Men and women process situations differently. For example, you will find that the communication between two men is very different than the communication between two women. Men process things externally; therefore, they talk about what they've seen. Two men may talk about sports, the news or a family situation. Women process things internally and will often talk about external situations, but their main focus will be on how those situations made them feel. When a husband and a wife disagree, their focuses are oftentimes different. A man will argue about the obvious. He may express his disdain at his wife's tone, her reason for arguing or the argument itself. A wife will argue about the not-so-obvious things that are contending with her mind. Instead of arguing about the obvious, women often argue about how their husbands actions or words made them feel. That is to say that a woman's thoughts are very important

As a Woman Thinketh

to her; therefore, in order for a man to truly have peace in his home, he must first understand his wife's way of thinking. He must value her thoughts as much as she does because her thoughts were deeply considered by her, built by her and sent out with expectation. A woman's thoughts are like children to her. When a man does not respect his wife's way of thinking, he does not respect his wife, for her thoughts are her, and she is her thoughts. Every one of a woman's thoughts is filled with substance, whether that substance is love, her fears or her dreams. Her husband must dissect her thoughts so that he can understand what to do with them. Communication is very important. You have to listen to God so you can hear and understand with compassion what your wife is saying.

A woman will always be complex to any man not permitted by GOD to have her. That's because a woman's thoughts are locked up in her heart and can only be released by GOD in due season. At the same time, only her GOD-permitted husband can unlock the wholeness of her and truly understand who she is, because he was granted permission by GOD to know the mystery of her. To understand his own wife, every man must take the time to get to know his wife's thought process. He needs to know how she thinks, why she thinks the way that she thinks, and how to change her mind when it needs to be changed. In studying and learning his wife, a husband will visit a sacred place that will change how he views his wife and how he treats her. When a man knows the heart of a woman, he will value or devalue the woman because he will have uncovered the most hidden part of her. He will have seen her without her skin; he will have seen the spirit of the woman that he chose to marry, and this experience is one that will change him forever. Oftentimes, when a wife is being argumentative towards her husband, it is because she wants him to see her as she is, but if it is not his season to uncover the wholeness of her, he will be blind to the obvious. No amount of discord or threats will open his eyes to see what GOD has hidden from him. A man's eyes can only see what he has worked for, because a man will only value what he has earned. Because women are loving creations of GOD, they want to freely give themselves wholly to their husbands, but GOD won't allow this because HE knows how HE designed men to operate. A man has to work for knowledge; he must search for wisdom, and he must ask for understanding. If he gets these treasures any other way, he cannot and will not respect them; nevertheless, if he obeys GOD and is granted permission to get this inside view of his wife at a whole new depth, he will not only obtain favor from GOD, he will maintain being favored by GOD.

Always remember to build your wife up with substance that cannot be taken away from her. The more positive words you sow into your wife, the more you will experience the depths of who she is and the width of her potential. As a husband, you should know that what you have seen with your wife is not the final product of your wife. There is so much in her that love will bring out of her, but it takes time, patience, persistence, love and the WORD of

GOD to draw it out of her.

Studying Your Wife

Every wife has her own way of thinking. You will find that what one woman considers a giant is a dwarf to another. That's why a husband has to know and understand his own wife, and to do this, he must learn to love his wife as he loves himself. He must see his wife as he sees himself. Whatever giant a husband sees standing before his wife is a giant standing before him. He has to be willing to take on her giants and bind up every thought that is not in line with the Word of GOD. This is because any problem that enters a man's house will act as a strongman against his family. Merriam-Webster Dictionary defines strongman as: *one who leads or controls by force of will and character or by military methods*. Anything that is distracting your wife is controlling your wife by force. Just as you would not allow another man to come in and take over your home, you cannot allow a devil or a mindset to come in and take over your home. In order for a problem to become a giant in your home, you must first become a dwarf. This means that you will be a slave to that problem. Mark 3:27 reads, *"No man can enter into a strong man's house, and spoil his goods, except he will first bind the strong man; and then he will spoil his house."* That is to say that whatever issues come into a man's house must first bind or imprison the man of that house. After that, those issues will spoil his house. To spoil his house means to take away everything that is valuable in that home.

In studying your wife, you will learn her way of thinking and her pattern of thinking. This is one of the greatest feats a man can achieve, because in knowing his wife, he will know how to maintain peace in his home. If a man does not know his wife, he will automatically open the door to strife and everything that strife brings with it. *"For where envying and strife is, there is confusion and every evil work" (James 3:16).*

Just how does one study his own wife? It's not as easy as it sounds. To study his wife, a man must first study the Word of GOD to better understand the roles of a wife. This way, when a wife is not operating in her role, he will know when and how to address the issue. At the same time, a man must study the Word of GOD to better understand his responsibility as a husband. That way, when he is not operating in his role, he will not address the wife, he will address himself. To study one's own wife is imperative to a marriage's success. After all, there are many wicked men out there who will patiently and effortlessly study a man's wife from the outside and learn more about her than the husband who lives inside the house with her. They do this as an attempt to seduce a woman outside of her marriage, and out from under the covering of CHRIST. Therefore, it is very important for a husband to know his own wife so that he can protect his wife from the wiles of the devil. To study her, he must speak

Studying Your Wife

with her often. To study her, he must listen intently to the abundance of her heart because a woman is not what a man sees; a woman is the heart in which a man hears.

A woman's facial expressions will always give a man the first indication as to what is going on in the mind of his wife. You will find that at times, a woman will say that there is nothing wrong with her, but her expressions will alert you to the presence of an unwanted thought. Many women believe that they can deal with these thoughts alone, and in many cases, they can; nevertheless, there are some attacks that require WORD attention. Again, as a husband, you are the strongman and you must remain the strongman of your house; otherwise, another strongman (devil) will sit at the head of your table.

To study one's own wife, a husband must learn her habits, her strengths and her weaknesses. A watchful husband can keep peace in his home much more than a distracted husband.

- **Her Habits:** Every wife has a habit. A habit is a pattern of behavior, and these patterns of behavior are manifestations of her thought patterns. Many arguments that start in a marriage surface because of minor issues such as the misplacement of the car keys. Most women have a built-in photographic memory; therefore, they tend to memorize the habits of their husbands. Nevertheless, every woman has a habitual behavior for every mood she enters. For example, when she's at peace, she may habitually put the car keys on the stand next to the door, but when she's stressed, she may habitually toss the keys onto the couch. If you know her calm behaviors and her not-so-calm behaviors, you'll know where to look for misplaced keys or any other misplaced items in your home. At the same time, you will know when something is bothering her without her ever telling you. Knowing your wife's habits will help you to create a mental dictionary of who she is, what she does and how each behavior is to be defined.

- **Her Strengths:** Every woman has strengths, and these strengths are areas where she has been refined by the trials of life. It is a mistake for a husband to underestimate the strength of his spouse, especially in those areas where she is strongest. In knowing her strengths, a husband will learn to trust his wife and let her show him how valuable she is. One of the errors that many men make is trying to flex their own strength, and pridefully trying to cover the strength of their wives. A woman who is encouraged to flex the wisdom that GOD has given her is the same woman who is encouraged to grow stronger in the LORD.

- **Her Weaknesses:** Just as every woman has strengths, every woman has weaknesses. Weakness in a woman is not always a defect in that woman. Oftentimes, it is the evidence of her past and the reflection of her future.

Studying Your Wife

Wherever she is weak, GOD will eventually strengthen her. As a husband, your responsibility is to cover her in those areas and encourage her strength in the LORD. There are so many husbands who encourage the growth of these weak areas so they can feel needed and wanted by their wives, but this is never a good idea. Keep in mind that as a husband, you may not always be around to protect her in those areas. If she's left alone with your children, and she does not know how to cope without you, not only will she be exposed to the dangers of this world, but your children will be exposed to those dangers as well. A woman's weakness can be her fears, for example. If a woman came from a broken home where no man was present, she may fear being abandoned. When she feels threatened in that area, she may overreact because of her fear. A husband should never deal with the reaction; he should always deal with the fear.

There are some initial tidbits that you should learn about your wife before marrying her, and they include: her favorite color, her most desired dreams, the type of husband she wants, the type of husband she does not want, how many children she hopes to have, how she plans to mother those children and so on. You learn these things so that you won't repeatedly cross those boundaries that she has set up in her heart. At the same time, if those boundaries were set up by her fears, you will know what strongman needs to be overcome in her life. You would then share that very same information about yourself with her, because the two of you are one person. As one person in CHRIST, the two of you will merge your dreams together, and you can help to extinguish the fears of one another.

As a husband, you should also know the lineage and strongholds of your wife's predecessors. Even though we are saved by the Blood of the Lamb, the flesh is still our weakest area. This is why we are called to walk after the spirit and not the flesh; nevertheless, we will often default to our flesh when we don't know how to handle a situation spiritually. In learning the strongmen of her family's lineage, you will know how to come against generational thinking because you will know what keeps coming against your marriage. For example, a wife who has come from a lineage of chaos and divorce may see divorce as a way to defeat any Goliath that enters her marriage. With a woman like this, a husband has to be patient, loving and reassuring. Additionally, he has to bind up the strongman of divorce and help his wife to embrace a new way of thinking.

Put your signature on her, not just your last name. You do this by learning the little things that make her smile. A husband is like a treasure hunter. His job is to find every smile that is hidden in his wife. There are some routes that you know, and there are some trails that you will have to blaze yourself. You don't always have to do something grand or spend a lot of money. Women just like to know that they are loved and that they are appreciated. Just telling your wife that she is beautiful to you is a powerful gesture that bears so much force that she'll use it to slap any devil that tells her otherwise. Endearing gestures like holding her hands or putting your arm around her are potent enough to send seven devils to flight. Long walks at the park are treasured by most women. Even the way a man looks at his wife is appreciated by his wife when she sees sparks in his eyes.

You'll find many men who will contentiously protest, "But what about what a man needs?! Why can't the wife study her husband so she can be a better wife to him?!" One of the things I have learned over the course of my marriage is that in striving to make my wife happy, I have found happiness for myself. You see, any man who delivers a smile must first possess a smile. When a man brings a smile out of his wife, there is something that happens to him in that moment. In that instance, he will discover something so huge, it had to be hidden in plain sight. That is, he will discover that his happiness is directly linked to her happiness.

The Tests of Marriage

A test is an opportunity to develop, and it is an opportunity to try out what you have learned over the length of your marriage. There are the tests that try us to see how much we know the Word, and there are the tests that try us to see just how much we know our wives. We are all tested in this thing we call life, and tests are rarely ever fun. Sometimes, we are tested by trials and tribulations, and other times, we are tested by our own ways of thinking. Regardless of what we are tested by, we have to pass the test to embrace a whole new level in our lives.

In the marriage setting, there are two people who have come together as one person; nevertheless, both people have individual

The Tests of Marriage

dreams. The husband's dream may be to move to Florida and spend out the rest of his days enjoying relaxing days at the beach. The wife's dream, on the other hand, may be to move to Alaska and spend out her days skiing on the snow banks. With such conflicting plans, an argument is inevitable; therefore, GOD allows both parties to be tested so their minds will change. HE doesn't want division in the marriage setting. At the same time, our plans for ourselves aren't always HIS plans for us. The tests often bring us into a place of humility; a place where we are forced to confront ourselves, reflect on our very own steps and how we have deviated from following GOD'S path for us. As we mature in CHRIST, we often find that our plans change, our desires change and our minds change. This tells us that the tests are necessary for the testimonies.

When a man takes on the role of a husband, he becomes a student to marriage. The very minute he quotes his vows to his new bride, the bell rings and he begins to receive lesson

The Tests of Marriage

behind lesson. Following each lesson is a test, and following each test is a testimony or complaint; it depends on how the matter is handled. A new husband will often fly through his lessons initially because he is enjoying the perks of marriage life. He has not yet encountered the waves that crash against marriages during the storms of life. In the first few months, he will happily wear his new title of "husband" and dote on his wife. After the honeymoon stage is over, reality begins to set in. Marriage isn't just a love party that never ends; marriage is responsibility. Marriage requires work and lots of it. Responsibility wouldn't be so scary if every man knew what to do; after all, a man will happily fix whatever he knows how to fix just to show his skill. But there are no physical tools available to fix a marriage or mend a broken heart. There are no vacuums in existence that will make the ugly words said during a fight disappear. There are no remote controls to put an angry wife on mute, or to rewind back to happier days. There are no eject buttons on a wife that a man can push to remove whatever problems that have gotten into her heart. Instead, there is the Word of GOD, and there are alternatives to the Word, but we know those alternatives don't work in our favor. What we have before us is a problem that cannot be fixed with mere hands. It requires a strength far stronger than what the flesh offers; it requires wisdom, and wisdom requires that you are tested.

In the previous chapter, we talked about the importance of studying one's wife. A husband will oftentimes find himself tested by his wife or others in relation to his wife. Let's say that you are married to a beautiful and vivacious woman who you know very little about because you haven't truly studied her. One day, you're out on the town having a great time with one another. You have gone out to eat, taken her to the mall, and now the two of you are relaxing at the ice cream parlor in the mall. All of a sudden, a group of beautiful immoral women passes you by. One of the women stops to flirtatiously wave at you, and you smile and wave back, just trying to be polite. The group of women walk away laughing, but now you

The Tests of Marriage

have a new problem on your hands. Your wife has just been disrespected; all the while you were being flattered. For you, the issue doesn't seem like such a big deal, but for your wife, it's bigger than Texas. What just happened was you were tested, and you failed the test. If you had studied your wife, you would know what the true issue is. Most men would accuse their wives of being insecure if they found themselves in this situation, but insecurity is not the real issue here. The issue is: You allowed your wife to be disrespected, and you did not correct the one who disrespected her. Instead, you mishandled your wife's feelings because you truly did not know that this would be an issue, or you didn't know it would be that big of an issue. In this moment, you should have stood by your wife. The correct way to handle such an issue is to firmly say, "Hello to you from me AND my wife."

How much do you know your wife? If you were tested tomorrow about the little things, would you pass or fail the test? To know the answer to this, try asking yourself a few questions that you should know the answer to. Better yet, check with your wife to see if she'd be willing to ask you some questions about her. If you fail the test, it may not be so offensive to her, seeing as you are attempting to get to know her better. Do you know the feel of your wife's hands? If you were blindfolded, would you be able to differentiate between her hands and the hands of another woman? Do you know her body's temperature when she is upset or when she is joyful? If you were in a dark place, and you were required to feel the faces of five women, would you know which face belonged to your wife? Most men won't know this because we are taught to provide for our families more than we are taught to know our families.

Paternity & Maternity Tests

In marriage, you will fight about issues both big and small. There will be times when you are wrong, and there will be times when your wife is wrong. How you handle those times will determine how time handles you over the course of your marriage.

Every problem that enters your marriage has a parent. Either you are the father of that problem, your wife is the mother of that problem or the both of you have created it. Knowing where an issue was conceived is vital to the existence of a marriage, because any roots left planted will continue to grow. The issue isn't always what stems on the surface; oftentimes, the issue is the root and the size of that root. Consider the redwood tree. The largest known redwood tree is 379 feet tall, but before a tree can grow so tall, its roots have to grow bigger and root deeper so the tree will be able to stand. The lifespan of a redwood tree is generally five to seven hundred years, even though some redwood trees have survived for more than two thousand years. Imagine whatever problem you encounter in your marriage as a redwood tree. Because of its lifespan, that problem could effortlessly outlive you. Because of its height, a redwood tree would easily tower over you in its youth. Because of the size of its roots, a redwood tree

The Tests of Marriage

is probably more grounded in dirt than many of us are in the Word of GOD. In order to destroy a redwood tree, the roots would have to be pulled up. Once a tree is chopped down, it won't often grow up again, but it will give life to any other plants around it. Marital problems behave in the same manner. If the root of an issue is not addressed, the problems will continue to grow and tower over your marriage. You may be able to remove the giant problem that you see, but if the root is still there, it may help sustain other problems in your marriage.

Most problems that enter marriage have a parent, and each problem needs to be tested so that it can be uprooted forevermore. For example, let's say that the husband is extremely jealous about his wife. He does not like other men talking to her, and he does not approve of most of her friends. Because of his stand, the couple argues a lot and the marriage is in trouble. They go to a marriage counselor to seek advice, but the husband does not like what he hears. It appears that the marriage counselor is pointing fingers at him, but in his mind, his wife is the issue. If she'd only stop talking to her male co-workers, everything would be fine. He is the father of that problem, and until he understands this, he won't be able to deal with it. Consequentially, his jealousy may be the very poison that ends the life of his marriage. If he were to realize that he is responsible for the issues in his marriage, he may seek help and make a change for the better. If he never recognizes his faults, he would continue to sow more seeds and not recognize them as his own.

The fastest way to rid your home of a problem is to address it head-on and to be honest about your own faults. As your marriage matures, you will find that when you accept responsibility for your failures, your wife will learn to accept responsibility for her failures. Pride won't sit at the head of your table, and unforgiveness won't spoon with your wife while you lay a few feet away consciously trying to make sure that your legs don't touch hers. Every test that you endure should be followed up with prayer and followed through with obedience. Every argument that you have should be examined, and the root of the issue should be plucked up. After all, our marriages are very similar to our relationships with the LORD. The very same issues that threaten our relationships with our wives are the issues that threaten our relationships with the LORD. Oftentimes, the strongman is pride. This is the very reason GOD said that our prayers would be hindered if we did not honor the wives of our youth. Any manifestation of a divide we have with our wives reflects a divide in our relationships with the LORD. We have to remain truthful with ourselves so that we can honor HIM by honoring her, and we can honor her by honoring HIM.

A test does not indicate that you have married the wrong woman. Sometimes, a test indicates that you are entering a new season in your ministry, life and marriage, and you are being tried to see if you can fit together as one in the next level. After all, GOD does not want to elevate you if elevation is going to divide your home, since marriage is your first ministry. HE will allow you to be tested at the level that you are to try you out for the next dimension, because the devils that will challenge you at the next level outrank the devils that challenge you at your current level. If you can't handle those marriage imps today, how can you overcome tomorrow's giants?

He Say, She Say

We think that all of our tests will come from the enemy; therefore, we will have those times where we are consciously battling with him. But what many don't know is that a lot of the tests we endure will come from our wives as well.

Women are unique creatures who are oftentimes more sensitive to the direction their marriages are heading in than men. As husbands, we simply ride through each day with our wives and children in tow. Our wives, on the other hand, don't simply ride through the days; they watch the road in front of us and tell us when they believe we have made a wrong turn. Of course, we don't like to receive directions from our wives, so we'll keep traveling down the same roads over and over again, hoping to find our way back to the main roads. This opens up the door to conflict, and we've got to learn how to put pride aside and let our wives be who they are: our help meets.

Think about a road trip. During a road trip, you will find that you have the following tools:

- What you know. (Your knowledge).
- What your wife knows. (Her knowledge).
- The Bible. (Your map).
- The HOLY SPIRIT. (Your G.P.S. System).
- Your Pastor. (Your traffic signs).
- Your pride. (That man on the side of the road who gives you the wrong directions or tells you how to go the long way).

During this road trip, your wife falls asleep often but wakes up to ask you a series of questions. She's trying to determine where you both are and how long it will take before you arrive at your destination. These questions are welcomed when you know that you have advanced in your journey while she was asleep. These questions are not welcomed when you feel lost and you are trying to figure out how to get back to the main road. The main road, of course, is what you know and what you are familiar with.

Your wife is asking questions because she wants to know where you are and if her assistance is needed. Over the course of our marriages, our wives will ask us questions because they want to know if the marriage is advancing, if our hearts are retreating and if their assistance is needed in repairing any damaged areas of the marriages.

In this chapter, we will talk about the common questions and comments made by women during a marriage and how we ought to respond. Remember Proverbs 15:1: *"A soft answer turns away wrath: but grievous words stir up anger."* Below are ten questions commonly asked by women, the wrong responses and the right responses.

1. **"Do you still love me?"** Every husband will become familiar with this question, but many of them will not answer it properly. To us, the obvious answer is "yes", but to a woman, it goes much deeper than that. A simple "yes" from us will often be met by a long speech from our wives detailing why they felt prompted to ask this question. Women often ask these questions when they feel unloved or they don't see the show of affection from you that they are accustomed to getting. Don't become offended by the question. She simply needs reassurance.

   Wrong Response: "Yes, I still love you. Why?"

   Right Response: "Yes, I still love you. I think about you every day, and I thank GOD for you. You are the only woman in this world for me, and I thank GOD for creating you for me. If you are ever in doubt, let me apologize because it means that I haven't told you or I haven't showed you just how much I love you.

You are forever my wife and forever my baby."

2. **"Did you miss me today?"** This question is often asked by a woman who wants to dive into a romantic moment, not a contentious one. Women love the highs associated with loving words; therefore, such questioning is oftentimes their attempts to "light a spark."
   Wrong Response: "I see you every day. How can I miss you?"
   Right Response: "Of course I missed you. Can't you tell? I am always happy when I see my beautiful wife."

3. **"Is she prettier than I am?"** This is a question that some women ask during the youth of their marriages, but as they mature, this line of questioning will likely cease. The right response can terminate this question entirely.
   Wrong Response: "She is who she is and you are who you are."
   Right Response: "Baby, I don't know why you feel that you need to compete

with other women or why you need to feel validated when you feel intimidated. You are more than beautiful to me and that's why I married you. I don't like questions like this because they set the wrong mood, when all I want you to feel is loved, appreciated and beautiful. You are who I chose, and I do not regret marrying you."

4. **"So she found out that her husband was cheating on her, and now they are divorcing."** Even though this isn't a question, it is an attempt by your wife to get answers from you as to what you would do. She basically wants to know if she's in danger of suffering the same fate that the subject of her communication is suffering. Never blame the wife; it'll only detonate her fears.
Wrong Answer: "You don't know what's going on in their marriage, sweetie."
Right Answer: "That's sad. Well, we have to keep praying for them, and don't worry: I could never do that to you. I

love you too much."

5. **"Do you think I'm fat?"** This infamous question has sparked many fights, hurt feelings and insecurities. Truthfully, the only right answer is the truth told in love, even though it may not be received well either way. After all, if your wife is obese, you have to love her enough to help her get to a healthy size.
Wrong Answer: "How much do you weigh now?"
Right Answer If She's Not Obese: "No, you are not fat. Baby, you are beautiful to me as you are."
Right Answer if She is Obese: "Baby, I love you and I don't want you to be insecure about your appearance. Whatever your size is and will be, I will always love you and stay by your side. To answer your question, you are overweight, but it doesn't change how I feel about you. I want us both to go to the gym, because I want you to be around for a long time."

6. **"So, what do you like about being**

married to me?" Again, this is one of those questions designed to spark an intimate moment. Your wife does not expect a negative answer, and it is the chance to set the mood for a really positive day.

Wrong Answer: "I like everything about you."

Right Answer: "I love coming home to you. I love the way you look, the way you smell, the way you walk and even how you talk. When I come home and see your beautiful face, I realize that I am blessed to have you. If I have had a bad day, your smile makes me forget everything bad that's happened that day. You are like sunshine peeking through my clouds, and I love you."

7. **"Tell me what you think I need to change."** Beware of this question. Oftentimes, this question is coming from a wife who feels that your affections towards her have changed, and she's trying to determine where the both of you took that wrong turn. Either way,

when this question is asked, prepare for a long discussion no matter how you respond. Sometimes, you may be able to escape the long and drawn out exchange of words by simply offering a positive response and then asking your wife to bow her head so you can pray on the issue. Women oftentimes don't like to discuss things that have been given over to GOD.

Wrong Answer: "Truth be told, you need to change your attitude."

Right Answer: "We're both imperfect creatures, baby, and we are just learning one another. I believe you need to work on your temper, and I need to work on my _____, but we'll do this together in love. Let's pray about it now."

8. **"Do you remember what you said to me the first time we met? Do you remember what I was wearing the first time we kissed?"** This is another one of those questions designed to spark the mood, but it oftentimes takes

a wrong turn when the man does not remember what his wife has remembered.

Wrong Answer: (Any lie told is the wrong answer).

Right Answer: "Baby, I have had so many amazing days with you, and I can't recall them all. This doesn't mean that the day was any less special to me than it was to you. It simply means that while you were paying attention to the details of the day, I was distracted by the sight of you."

9. **"If I died, would you ever marry again?"** Don't panic. This question is often asked by a curious wife who is simply spending too much time in her thoughts. The wrong answer, however, could send her back to her thoughts to ponder on what you said, and we don't want this.

   Wrong Answer: "Yes, indeed. I love being married."

   Right Answer: "If GOD told me to, yes, I would remarry."

10. **"What are you thinking about?"**

    Women often worry about what they cannot see. Your thoughts are your private thoughts, and not knowing what they are scares some women. At the same time, women are naturally curious creatures.

    Wrong Answer: (Any lie told is the wrong answer).

    Right Answer: (Any truth told is the right answer.) Avoid telling her anything that you know would upset her. For example, "I saw my ex today at the store, and I was just wondering why she winked at me when she walked off." To avoid upsetting your wife when your thoughts aren't lined up properly, simply return the question with, "What are you thinking about?"

Always remember that men and women are different, and there are some behaviors that are characteristic to each gender. Don't put too much though into your wife's line of reasoning. Instead, be sure to reassure her when she needs it, to encourage her when she needs encouraging, and to correct her when she needs correcting.

Sowing Seeds In Your Marriage

We were taught to sow seeds into our ministries and the ministries of others. We were taught to sow seeds into the lives of those who need help. We were taught to sow seeds into the desires of our flesh. When we are hungry, we have no problem or second thoughts about eating. Nevertheless, most of us were never taught the importance of sowing seeds into our marriages. Instead, when you talk with the average couple about sowing seeds in marriage, their minds go directly to sex and the fruit of sex. Marriage is our first ministry. How can a man lead a congregation if he cannot lead his home?

Every word you speak to your wife is a seed. Every seed, if not uprooted, will produce a harvest. When you speak blessings to your wife, she will bless you. When you speak reproachfully to your wife, strife will step in, and the Bible tells us that every evil thing comes with strife. Therefore, as husbands, we have to learn to send out the good words and cast down the wrong ones. When we are angry with our wives, it is not easy for us to say what we truly need; instead, we say what we feel. But we have to remember that our feelings come from our flesh; nevertheless, our spirit man intercedes for us by telling the LORD what we need. Galatians 5:16-17 reads, *"This I say then, Walk in the Spirit, and ye shall not fulfil the lust of the flesh. For the flesh lusteth against the Spirit, and the Spirit against the flesh: and these are contrary the one to the other: so that ye cannot do the things that ye would."* Let's rightly divide the scriptures. **What does it mean to walk in the Spirit and not fulfill the lust of the flesh?** To walk in the Spirit is to walk in the will of GOD. It means to obey GOD, walk in faith and not follow after how you feel. We have to understand that we were taught to walk in the flesh from the very day we took our first steps. Our parents encouraged us to learn to be self-sufficient. Many of us were taken to church, but we were still flooded with information about how to walk after the flesh. Now, our Father in Heaven is teaching us to walk all over again after HIS SPIRIT. So we have to start all over again as babies in CHRIST and learn to walk in accordance with the Word of GOD.

The flesh is nothing but meat. It is our earth suit, our permission to live in the realm of the earth; but once we leave this earth, we do not take our flesh with us. This means that we are not our flesh, and our flesh is not who we are. Our flesh is simply our personal dwellings. Think about your physical house. You live in it, but it is not alive. You are the life in that house, and because you are there, your house will be made alive when you are home. Once you leave your house, it cannot turn its own lights on or off. Your house cannot clean itself, nor can it warm itself up in the winter months. The same goes for your flesh. Your flesh is only made alive by the presence of your spirit, but once your spirit is gone, your flesh will not live.

For this reason, GOD warns us not to be led by our flesh.

What does it mean to lust against the Spirit? TheFreeDictionary.com defines lust as:
a. An overwhelming desire or craving: a lust for power.
b. Intense eagerness or enthusiasm.

To lust against the Spirit means that the flesh desires to take the place of the Spirit. Our flesh is constantly battling it out with the LORD for control. Our flesh desires to take the place of our spirit man, because our spirit man is led of the LORD.

What are the lusts of the flesh? Galatians 5:19-21 answers this question for us. *"Now the works of the flesh are manifest, which are these; Adultery, fornication, uncleanness, lasciviousness, Idolatry, witchcraft, hatred, variance, emulations, wrath, strife, seditions, heresies, Envyings, murders, drunkenness, revellings, and such like: of the which I tell you before, as I have also told you in time past, that they which do such things shall not inherit the kingdom of God."*

The flesh desires to do the works of death, for the flesh does not have an inheritance of everlasting life with GOD.

Why can't you do the things that you "would" or want to do? It's only natural that you want to sin, for the sin nature of the flesh is strong. Instead, you must follow after the Spirit and do the works of the Spirit, even when your flesh demands otherwise. Just as the flesh has fruits, the Spirit has fruits. Galatians 5:22-24 reads, *"But the fruit of the Spirit is love, joy, peace, longsuffering, gentleness, goodness, faith, Meekness, temperance: against such there is no law. And they that are Christ's have crucified the flesh with the affections and lusts."*

Think about the seeds of the flesh and the seeds of the Spirit. Each seed is fertile and will produce fruit after its own kind. Galatians 6:8 confirms this: *"For he that soweth to his flesh shall of the flesh reap corruption; but he that soweth to the Spirit shall of the Spirit reap life everlasting."* Remember, your flesh is your temporary house, but your spirit man is everlasting. Your spirit man will never die; it is an eternal force. When you are sowing love, joy, peace, longsuffering, gentleness, goodness, faith, meekness and temperance, you are sowing into your eternal state. Your spirit man has dominion over your flesh; therefore, by sowing into your eternal being, you cause your flesh to have to line up with the Word you serve. It goes without saying; however, when you are sowing the works of the flesh, you will reap death.

Many times we will notice that our wives aren't speaking the way we want them to speak, and they aren't doing the things we want them to do. As husbands, we will patiently excuse this behavior for a few days, but our grace isn't as extensive as GOD'S grace. After our limitations are reached, we may respond by being argumentative, by leaving the house or by cutting off our feelings; otherwise known as emotional starvation. A woman does not know how to function when she is starved emotionally, and most men know this. But in shutting down our feelings and becoming cold towards our wives, we not only dishonor the women GOD has entrusted us with, we dishonor GOD, HIMSELF! Instead of arguing, complaining or playing mind games, we must see our lives and marriages as gardens. If we don't like what's growing up, we have to pluck it up and sow better seeds. This isn't easy to a man being led by his flesh, because our flesh tells us to fight it out until the end. After all, wrath and strife are fruits of the flesh.

Another seed we must sow in our marriages are good deeds. Every good deed deserves another one. When you make a habit of sewing good seeds, GOD will make a habit of blessing you. The Bible refers to the wife as the crown of her husband. There is nothing in the earth greater than watching your crown sparkle. At the same time, when she sparkles, she makes you look good. Anyone that sees her knows that she is polished and that she belongs to someone because she's been well taken care of. When people see her, they should also be able to tell that she is the wife of a man of GOD, because your light will merge with her light to create an illumination so bright that she'll light up the room everywhere she goes. You'll hear a lot of worldly women say to their friends that they are glowing. This usually means that joy is radiating through the woman, and this joy is believed to have come from the presence of a "decent" man. We are the Body of CHRIST, and the Bible calls us to be "good" men; therefore, the light that is in us comes from the LORD. It is a pure light; one that is the evidence of the presence of GOD. It's not fleshly given, even though HIS light will radiate through our whole being.

What are some good deeds that we can sow into our marriages? Below, I have listed ten habits we need to embrace.

1. Buy roses and hand them to her. A lot of men buy roses and leave them on the dining room or living room table, but this act takes the intimacy from the gesture. When buying roses, always hand them to your wife and tell her why you

purchased them.

2. Date her often. It's a well-known fact that women love to get dressed up and be seen. Women love to have any excuse to beautify themselves because it makes them feel important, loved and alive. Date her at least once a week.

3. Court her every day. The worst thing a husband can do is stop courting his wife. Courting the wife will actually help you to stay interested in her, and it'll help her to remain in love with you. Flirt with her and tell her how beautiful she is to you.

4. When away from her, call her just to hear her voice.

5. Take her out of the country (or at least the state) yearly if you can.

6. Cook special dinners for her sometimes. A loving candlelit dinner says a lot to a woman.

7. Be spontaneous. Women often grant access to themselves intimately when

their minds have been triggered by loving, spontaneous acts. Any man who doesn't surprise his wife slowly becomes a trespasser in her sights. Show me a monotone husband, and I'll show you a man whose wife has a "no trespassing" sign on her body.

8. Make every moment count. Always tell your wife that you love her, and always be prepared to show it as well.

9. Take her shopping sometimes. For most women, shopping is therapy. Put a shopping budget together and take her out on a shopping spree every now and again. Then, give her thirty-minutes to happily discuss with you why she purchased what she purchased.

10. Kiss her while she sleeps. Believe it or not, she will remember.

Of course, these gestures are common sense gestures that most good men, and some decent men, will embrace; nevertheless, as our marriages age, we tend to forget the little seeds that grew into big smiles. We can never allow ourselves to become slothful in our marriages. We can never allow ourselves to get so comfortable that we forget that our marriages need to be nurtured.

Every choice you make in your marriage is a seed sown into how your wife feels. There are some choices you'll make that will trigger that beautiful smile she has, and there are some choices you'll make that will trigger a waterfall of tears. In giving you her heart, she has given you the keys to how she feels. You have the power to make her day or ruin it. This is intimate access to one of the most sacred parts of her: her heart.

When she gave you her heart, it was likely during a time when you kept sowing the right words in her mind and showing her the things she wanted to see. You bought her roses, took her out on breath-taking dates, told her how beautiful she was, and you were very expressive in relation to how you felt about her.

Now that you are married to her, she rarely sees roses unless it's for a special occasion. Your dates to her now involve a drive-through window and a budget; the only compliments she gets from you is during sex, and how you feel about her is now a secret. Now you have a sense of entitlement to her, and you feel that she should be appreciative of you because you stuck it out with her through the highs and lows of her attitude.

A woman's attitude is not a reflection of who she is; it is oftentimes an expression of what's going on in her mind or her heart. Her mind is where all of today's, yesterday's and tomorrow's traffic flows. Her heart is like an open freeway or a traffic jam, depending on what's in it. Because you are her husband, you are always in her heart, meaning you can change the course of her day by simply doing the right things, saying the right words and helping her to remove any negative thing that's locked up in her heart. As the husband, you are always on her mind. This means that you have direct access to her thoughts, and you can change them by encouraging her throughout the day. All you have to do is sow the right seeds in her mind so they will find their way into her heart. What gets into her heart changes the very thought process of a woman; it changes her life.

Every day, you ought to invest in a smile from your wife and joy in your wife. What's the difference? A smile is an external representation of one being pleased with the thoughts going on in their minds. Joy is an internal condition that radiates externally. Joy is the evidence of the presence of GOD within a person.

1 Thessalonians 3:9-10- "For what thanks can we render to God again for you, for all the joy wherewith we joy for your sakes before our God; Night and day praying exceedingly that we might see your face, and might perfect that which is lacking in your faith?"

Psalms 43:4- "Then will I go unto the altar of God, unto God my exceeding joy: yea, upon the harp will I praise thee, O God my God."

Romans 15:13- "Now the God of hope fill you

with all joy and peace in believing, that you may abound in hope, through the power of the Holy Spirit."

Understanding Your Wife

Who can understand his own wife? Women are complex creatures, and they are often on emotional highs or hormonal lows; therefore, a husband has to learn to remain steadfast when his wife starts to fluctuate. We must remember that the Bible tells us that women are the weaker vessels, and we are to give honor to them as such. We may not always understand them, but let's face it; we're not supposed to understand them, we are supposed to love and cover them. Trying to understand one another is the reason so many couples argue more than they speak sensibly. You won't always understand one another, and you won't always agree, but that's okay. The mature way to handle disagreements is to agree upon a solution. The Word of GOD should always be the first thing you turn to, but there are some situations that you won't have to open your Bible to mediate. A good example of this is if your wife wanted to vacation in Rome, and you wanted to vacation in Chile. The wrong way to try and resolve this dispute is to try to flex your authority as the head. The right way is to arrange a meeting with your wife, sit down and the two of you should go over the benefits of both countries. Don't end the meeting until you have both come to an agreement. Maybe you'll vacation in Rome this year, and Chile next year. Always come to a mutual understanding that you will meet together without arguing, the use of harsh tones and the use of hard words.

Every man can understand his wife as he truly gets to know who she is from the inside out. The error is in studying what grows on the surface without studying what's planted underneath the surface. For example, you will find that your wife may cook your favorite dish when she's happy and make you sandwiches when she is unhappy. The surface of the issue is what's evident: she cooks when she's happy, but she doesn't cook when she is unhappy. What is the root of the issue, however? What are her beliefs? You may find that she believes by not cooking that she is sending a clear message to you, and this way of thinking can cause some friction between the two of you. In this case, you would have to address her beliefs and offer her a better solution.

Your wife is different than any other man's wife. Women often have some ways in common, but each woman has her own personality, strongholds and desires. Trying to better understand the gender itself, rather than learning to understand your wife is wrong. As husbands, we have to understand the common ways of the female gender; nevertheless, we must learn to understand the peculiar ways of our own wives as well. One of the worst things I have ever witnessed men doing was comparing their wives to the wives of other men. Our wives have their own unique characteristics. They are individuals, but when compared to other women, we dishonor who they are and the GOD who created them as they are.

When you're at home watching television with your wife, you may have those moments where you are watching a show together, and the character wife on television may do and say some of the same things that your wife does and says. In these rare moments, you'll often notice that your wife may turn to look at you because at that moment, she feels validated. At the same time, you may laugh it off and consider that all women are just the same. These moments help to relieve any built-up tension between the two of you, but if this is the case, it only means that you have not yet gotten to know your wife. As men, we try to understand the gender more than we try to understand the individual. As we grow older and mature more, we learn to acquaint ourselves with the hearts of our wives more than the gender of our wives. That's why you will often find that older couples are more in sync with one another, and they don't fight nearly as much as younger couples. If younger husbands would embrace this truth, they could pass over all of those years of fruitless fighting and learn better ways of communicating with their spouses earlier on in their marriages. Oftentimes, couples wait until they are too old to fight anymore before they put their weapons away and learn civilized ways of communicating with one another.

How can you understand your wife? Of course, in the previous chapter, we discussed studying our wives, but there is another depth to it; one not explored by too many men. To get to this sacred place, we have to put away our jealousy, pride and impatience. What is this mysterious place? The depths of her heart. When women come together, they often reveal some of the most innermost parts of their hearts to one another. This is because they feel they can relate to one another, and they can share these hidden parts of themselves without feeling judged. When a wife is with her husband, on the other hand, she may hold back some of that information because she feels that her husband cannot relate to her, and she fears that he may judge her. For this reason, you'll notice that women tend to be closer to their friends. They can speak to one another in body language or just a quick look of their eyes. As remarkable as this is, it is also sad that in this day and age, many wives feel they cannot share the depths of who they are with the man they lie next to every night. Knowing your wife at a greater depth than her friends know her is absolutely necessary for the survival of a marriage. Think about it. What if you came home from work, entered your house, and your wife was standing afar off, and she gave you an eerie glare? Would you recognize the look? What if someone was in your home holding her at gunpoint, but you couldn't see them? Her friends may recognize that glare; they may recognize that something is obviously wrong. But for a man who has never learned to understand his wife, this look means that he is in trouble with her.

Understanding your wife means knowing what motivates her and what causes her to react positively and negatively. A woman who may have had a traumatic experience in deep water may overreact when in the presence of deep water. For example, if a woman had almost drowned as a child, she may fear swimming pools over three feet in depth. Understanding this is very important, so if she overreacts near deep water, her husband won't take it personal. Instead, he will know that fear has to be bound up, and he has to help his wife to get over this fear. In understanding her, he will be empathetic when others are being judgmental. In understanding her, he can be loving when she's not acting lovable.

I have come in contact with many men who were intimidated by the best friends of their wives. Why was this? It was more than likely because they recognized a connection between their wives and their wives' friends that they did not have with their wives. Even though the friend's connection is not a romantic connection, these guys were threatened by any bonds that appeared stronger than the bonds they had with their wives. In many of these situations, the threatened husbands demanded the end of the friendships and found justifiable reasons to stand against their wives' friends. In using poor judgment, they break up healthy friendships for unhealthy reasons. After all, the friend was not the real issue. The issue was the husband recognized that there was a depth to his wife that he had not yet explored, and he became jealous when he witnessed someone else exploring it, be they male or female. Instead of coming against these friendships, the proper response is to try to get to know one's own wife at that level, and even on a deeper level. There are always unexplored chambers of a woman's heart, many of those chambers not even known by her. Here are ten tips to help you to understand your wife and get to know her better:

1. Ask questions and be willing to listen. Most women are talkative, but they tend to spend too much time filling in the details whereas men want to get straight to the point. Sometimes, the diamond is in the details. Listen closely.

2. When asking questions, never become angry when the answer you receive is

Understanding Your Wife

not the answer you wanted. For example, many husbands ask their wives about previous relationships they were in before they'd met them. Of course, these women can openly talk to their friends about their past relationships, but in most cases, they can't share too much information with the husband. If you are bold enough to ask personal questions, be strong enough to deal with the answer. If your wife detects jealousy or anger, she may clam up and refuse to share any more information with you.

3. Never be judgmental or make your wife feel judged about your decisions, her past, or her plans. Understand that everything she was, everything she is and everything that she will be is a seed that was sown or will be sown. Take care of who she is, and you may be amazed at how she blossoms.

4. Always show interest, and don't go to sleep while she's talking! One thing women find insulting is a man dozing off

while they are talking. If you know your wife is a talker, and it ordinarily takes her an hour to get to the point, take her to the beach and let her share with you as you walk. You can also talk to her and ask her to get directly to the point in her stories. If you know your attention span is short, tell her. A good way to do this is to say, for example, "Baby, I love your stories, but can you get straight to the point when telling them to me? The issue is, I have an attention span that lasts five minutes or less. If you haven't gotten to the point in that time, you'll lose me. It's not an issue with you. The issue is I am not that good at listening for long periods of time."

5. Always give your wife feedback. A woman wants to know if you were listening, if you enjoyed her conversation, if you were bored by her conversation and how you feel about what she's said. Simple and short phrases often indicate that you aren't really listening, but giving your take on

the matter shows her that you were listening and are interested in what she's saying.

6. Give her an inside view of your heart. After all, this is what her friends do. It's nothing to be ashamed about, and your wife will love you for it.

7. Initiate some of the conversations. If your wife finds that she is the initiator of all verbal communications, she may feel that you don't like talking with her.

8. Find common ground. Your wife may have things that she likes to talk about, and you may have things you like to talk about. The way to mediate this is find something the both of you like to talk about.

9. Arrange a weekly note-writing session. Some people are more expressive on paper than they are face-to-face. You can incorporate a fun note-writing session to occur once a week or bi-weekly. During these sessions, the two of you are to write a note to one another

about how you feel, any issues you feel are plaguing the marriage and what you are hoping for.

10. Ask her what she wants in a husband as far as communication goes. In some cases, you may find that some women like things just the way that they are. They have "friend talk" reserved for their friends, and they have "couple talk" reserved for the two of you.

Remember, the key to better understanding your wife is communication. Not forced communication or lackadaisical communication; your wife needs open and friendly communication with you. Once you get past all of the things that make you uncomfortable communicating with her, you will likely find out so many wonderful things about her that you did not know. Oftentimes, these communications will rekindle the spark between the two of you that fizzled out years ago. In most cases, when a marriage begins to break down, it is because of lack of communication. The wife may feel misunderstood, and she may feel that her husband has no desire in getting to know her better. Of course, this could cause the both of you to develop a notion that trying to save the marriage is hopeless, and this is when most people begin to give up. This means that pride is at the forefront of their marriage's breakdown.

What I have found over the years is that many men are afraid of truly communicating with their wives. That's because many of us were taught that talkative men are effeminate. The truth is, it's good to talk, but it's better to listen. Women love feedback, and they love to be listened to. You don't have to be extremely chatty, but you can find a personal balance between talking and listening. Listening to your wife will help you to better understand her, relate to her and love her. Listening to your wife will serve as a reminder to you as to why you chose her to be your spouse. After all, a Godly woman is much more than what the eyes can see; a woman of GOD is like a deep well full of wisdom, blessings and surprises. Your love, communication and understanding will help to draw some gifts out of her that she didn't know were there! Oftentimes, these gifts are hidden in her, and she may not understand how to draw them out. What I have found out about many women is the fact that many of them have gifts they are conscious of, but something or someone has made them doubt those gifts. Something or someone has caused them to either put those gifts on the back-burner or deny those gifts. For this reason, your wife needs to be covered, protected and encouraged. When you come to the understanding of who your wife is and what gifts she has, you can go before the LORD and ask HIM how you can pull those gifts out of your wife. Sometimes, simple words of encouragement are enough. Sometimes, complimenting her works is enough. As the spouse, you need to know just what your wife needs to bring out the best of her. You'd be amazed at how happy and free your wife will become when you help her to release whatever has been dammed up in her. Always remember that the wife is a help meet. When you help her to be and remain free, she'll be free to help you.

Most women can be argumentative when they don't feel they are understood. At the same time, women often lose hope in relationships where they feel their husbands are not trying to understand them. Think about this: What if you were working at a company and giving them your all? You work harder than everyone that works there. You go that extra mile to show your superiors that you are appreciative of having the job and are deserving of promotion. You are often the first to come to work and the last to leave. The time for promotion comes up, and instead of the company promoting you, they promote one of your co-workers. The guy they chose to promote is often late for work. He rarely ever finishes his work assignments, and he's always doing just enough to get by. He is rude to his customers, and he is demeaning towards his superiors. He even complains about the job, often promising to walk away from the company as soon as another door opens for him. How would you feel to see him promoted over you? Most people would be upset, and they'd stop giving that company their all. Many would quit working for the company because their morale would go down, and it would be hard to sit in an environment where they don't feel appreciated. Women think the same way. A Godly woman will go that extra mile to show her husband that she loves him and appreciates him for choosing her to be his wife. She will wake up early to make sure that you and your children are off to work with a full belly. She will stay up late so she can tuck the children in and make sure you have whatever it is that you may need before you close your eyes. But if you ever make her feel as if all of her works are for nothing, her morale will go down. She'll lose whatever enthusiasm she had for that marriage because she feels it's all in vain. She does not ask for promotion; oftentimes, she simply wants to be acknowledged. Therefore, the wise thing for any husband to do is acknowledge his wife's sacrifices, but more than that, to show that he appreciates her for everything she does.

Try to understand your wife. To do this, you must get to know her the way she doesn't know herself. Women love when their husbands give them tours of their own ways; tours that they have never taken before. All the same, whatever you do for your wife, she will likely do for you in return. A happy and understood wife sets the atmosphere for a happy and understood husband.

Accept It: She's Right Sometimes

My military career was going great. I was promoted to sergeant (E-5) within the first two years in the Corps. When the time to reenlist came, I was given a lump sum bonus for my specialty of twenty-thousand dollars because of the type of work I did. When I received this money, Connie and I discussed investing it in the children's future. I was supposed to purchase government savings bonds for each child. It didn't go as planned, however, because I ended up talking with some investment companies. I thought that I'd found a quicker and easier way to increase or possibly double our investments in a few years. Of course, I was told that I could pull my original investment out at any time. You can pretty much guess what happened next. My

Accept It: She's Right Sometimes

agent invested my money into a mutual fund account that was supposed to turn a pretty good profit. Instead, my initial investment dropped from five thousand dollars to four hundred dollars within twelve months. I felt so stupid, and I was disappointed that I had let my family down. We struggled financially for a long time, barely making ends meet. I never consulted God or Connie to make that decision, and I ended up feeling like a fool.

There will be times when you will have two or more options to consider. These choices will stand before you asking you to choose the one you plan to go with. Being a man, you will want to make these decisions on your own to validate yourself as head of the house. Of course, this is pride, and pride always leads to the wrong choices being made. GOD called our wives "help meets". This means they are sent to help us, and we are to help them as we accompany one another in this life. When pride sets in you, GOD can't speak to you because you are too puffed up to hear HIM. Because of this, HE may speak to your wife so

Accept It: She's Right Sometimes

that she can help you to find your way back to a state of humility, and so you can take the route HE has designed for you. But when pride sets in, it's hard for us to hear anyone except ourselves. This is why we have to be conscious of the spirit we are operating in, and we have to be always aware of the fact that pride hunts a man the way a lion hunts a wounded calf.

One of the most harrowing and humbling realizations that I had to come to was that my wife was right more times than I gave her credit for. There were times when I was absolutely sure that I was making the right decisions, and I was unhappy that she was not standing with me on those decisions. Instead, she wanted to go in the opposite direction. This was upsetting because not only did I want her support, but I knew there was a possibility that she could be right. Like most men, I saw marriage the same way most children see video games. I thought I had to win, and if my wife had won more rounds than I did, she would become arrogant and want to take my

Accept It: She's Right Sometimes

place as the man of the house. I couldn't have that, so I kept making decisions and stumbling over my own choices. Ironically enough, "I" ended up losing many times, when "we" could have won had I trusted the wife GOD had blessed me with.

One of the common scenes you will find in many of Hollywood's love stories is a repentant husband who admits that he was wrong. During the movie, the husband played a cocky and prideful man who mistreated his wife and chased after his own glory. We saw his wife's pain, and we secretly wished that she would leave him. At the end of the movie, the husband was humbled and came to his wife humbly asking (or begging) for her forgiveness. If you'll look at your wife during those scenes, you may see teardrops or you may see her refusing to accept the character's apology, even though he's not apologizing to her. That's because pride is something women have to see each and every day that they are married. Let's face it: We can be some prideful creatures who wreak havoc on our marriages

Accept It: She's Right Sometimes

with our haughty looks. It's gotten so bad that Hollywood had to cast these men as legends to be admired for years to come.

Your wife is right sometimes. Your wife is right more times than you think she is. If you will look through the scriptures, you will find that GOD called wisdom "her." This was no accident on HIS part. GOD is like the husband, and wisdom is HIS wife. *"The LORD by wisdom has founded the earth; by understanding has he established the heavens" (Proverbs 3:19).* What would happen if GOD did not listen to HIS wisdom? After all, the two are one. GOD is wisdom, and wisdom is of GOD. You cannot separate GOD from HIS wisdom, and you cannot separate wisdom from her GOD. Wisdom is spiritual understanding. It is the very mind and heart of GOD.

When GOD blessed Solomon with wisdom, HE was giving him the knowledge of GOD. HE granted Solomon access to the very treasures

Accept It: She's Right Sometimes

of wisdom, and with this wisdom came the blessings of GOD. The same goes for our wives. What would happen if we did not listen to the wives GOD has given us? After all, we are one with them. Would you say that you trust the right side of your brain, but you don't trust the thoughts coming from the left side of it? Of course not. You don't know which directions your thoughts come from. What you know is that a thought has come in for you to consider. You must do the same with your wife. No man or thing can separate you from your wife, so it's better to take what she says into consideration and pray on it.

Agreeing to Disagree

Obviously, every couple disagrees, and that's okay. Some couples disagree loudly, while others disagree silently. Each couple has developed their own way of fighting; one that is unique to them, and one that is only understood by them. This is because every couple comes together with cultures they've picked up along their individual journeys in life, but they create a whole new culture once they are married to one another. Every couple's culture is a mixture of what they brought in from their upbringings, past relationships, future plans, understandings and misunderstandings. For this reason, you will notice that what triggers the parties in one relationship to fight won't often trigger another couple outside of that relationship. One man's pet peeve is another man's joke.

Most of us recognize that everyone outside of our homes is different and has the right to their own opinions; nevertheless, it's somewhat offensive for the spouse to have and enforce their own opinions. The truth is, the average husband thinks along these lines: "What I want is not bad. If my wife would only understand that I'm just trying to make a better future for us and our kids, we wouldn't have any issues." But the wife thinks the same way. She believes that if her husband would only understand what she's striving for, and he were to come on board, everything would work out past perfection. This line of thinking is selfish, even though the person with these thoughts has included their spouse in their plans. A lot of times, a spouse may not see his or her plans as selfish because they have included their spouse in their plans; nevertheless, any plans that come from self is selfish. It's no different than fornicating with the intent to marry. Many believers will engage in premarital relations with the hopes that their sexual rendezvous will lead to marriage. They believe that from within the marriage union, they could repent and live happily ever after with their spouses, but holiness just does not work that way. We can't say to GOD, "Let me sin first. I'm trying to sin my way into Your will, and after I get what I want, I'll give You what You want." This is the line of thinking of many husbands and wives, and this selfish mindset leads to constant bickering, divorce and bitterness. I've come across so many bitter people who will angrily proclaim that their estranged spouses were the reasons for their impending divorces. They explain that they had wonderful plans, but the other spouse had his or her own plans and would not bend. The real guilty parties in these cases are both parties, because neither one took the time out to consider that their individual selves were destroying the marriage. What they should have done was come up with a plan that involved both of their desires, but more than that, it should have involved GOD'S plan for their lives instead of their own plans.

When you met your wife, she had dreams. Women often start planning their happily ever afters when they are children, so their dreams are decades in the making. It's hard to get a woman to budge from a fantasy that is two or three decades old. As men, on the other hand, we didn't think too much about marriage as children. When we finally do consider marriage, it's oftentimes just something we have resolved ourselves to do. We look at the fact that we love the woman we intend to marry, she wants to get married and we don't plan on leaving her. To the average man, this is all the thought that he has put into marriage. So, when you come together as one person, you come in with individual realities and plans, and this is where the battle lines are drawn. The wife wants to talk and talk some more about the future, whereas the husband wants to talk about today. Our thoughts are: "What are we eating today? What are we doing today? What is she upset about today?" This means that we come into today physically as a couple, but mentally, we are often worlds apart. How can one resolve such an issue peacefully? It's obvious: sometimes, we have to agree to disagree.

Agreeing to Disagree

What does it mean to "agree to disagree?" Does this mean that we should be in opposition to one another, and agree that this is okay? Of course not. It means that we have to learn to respect one another's "me" for the sake of "us." Understand that your wife has plans, and some of them may come to pass, and some of them will never come to pass. This works the same way for you as well. But the better way to handle conflict is by coming together for prayer and asking GOD for HIS will to be done. Ask GOD to reveal HIS plans for the both of you, instead of trying to reason with one another. Whenever GOD begins to change your heart and your wife's heart, HE will mend your plans on one path where the two of you will be in agreement. But if you allow your flesh to make plans for your future, you are setting yourself up for a future of being alone.

What if your wife is insistent on having her way? She's planned long and hard to have a particular lifestyle, but you are not in agreement with her. Take a seat and talk with her, but bring the Word of GOD with you.

Agreeing to Disagree

Matthew 6:34 reads, *"Take therefore no thought for tomorrow: for tomorrow shall take thought of the things for itself. Sufficient unto the day is the evil thereof."* You simply bring the Word of GOD to the discussion, and explain to your wife that the two of you will follow the path that GOD has laid before you. Explain to her that wherever HE takes the both of you, you plan to be with her, love her and your desire is to see her happy. If she insists on speaking on the matter again and again, close the conversation with a loving message. Let her know that you will not discuss the issue with her anymore, but you will continue to pray on it. Of course, she may not be happy at your response, but understand that you are working towards the greater good for the both of you. Always try to speak on an issue, but when one party indicates that they are unmovable with the issue, exit the communication and try to end every talk on a friendly note. If the spouse is willing, exit the communication with a prayer, making sure to bind up pride either during the prayer together or whenever you are alone.

Agreeing to Disagree

Agreeing to disagree does not mean that the two of you are agreeing to be against one another. It means that you learn to respect the fact that each party has their own thoughts and plans. At the same time, always be aware of the fact that GOD is in control. Oftentimes, we worry that the other party may "win" and we'll end up holding the tab, but this isn't true if you stay in the will of GOD. Remind yourself of Proverbs 19:21: *"There are many plans in a man's heart; nevertheless the counsel of the LORD, that shall stand."* You will make plans; your wife will make plans, but only the plans of GOD will come to pass when you stand in faith instead of falling under fear. So, when your wife comes to you with her plans, the better thing to do is to tell her how you feel, but remind her of Proverbs 19:21. Always end all communications positively out of a show of respect for one another. This should be agreed on at the beginning of your marriage; that way, you won't find yourself being led into strife by your emotions. When you learn to respect your wife's differing opinions, she will learn to respect yours. Remember, as the husband, you set the stage for the atmosphere in your marriage and in your home. When things get too hot, it is often because selfishness has polluted your marriage.

When Divorce Looks Better Than Your Wife

What is divorce? In the world's system, divorce is the legal separation of two spouses; the termination of the marital vows. In the Word, however, divorce is only granted when one or both of the spouses have committed adultery or an unbeliever abandons his spouse. Outside of adultery, divorce is simply one or two selfish people who forgot that they were supposed to be one. The husband forgot to cleave to his wife, or the wife forgot to submit to her husband. In cleaving to his wife, the husband would honor, protect, cover and love her. To cover her, he would stay covered by CHRIST. To submit to her husband, the wife would simply speak to her husband about issues in their marriage. She would love him, and by submitting to him, she is in submission to his head, JESUS CHRIST. Divorce is always the evidence that someone is out of order. In many cases, it's just one of the spouses; in other cases, it's both spouses. We must understand that GOD called us one with our spouses, but the enemy will try to divide that one into two. He does this by encouraging selfishness. You will always know when the enemy has crept into the heart of one of the spouses because of the words they will use. *"For out of the abundance of the heart the mouth speaks" (Matthew 12:34).* Selfish questions and responses sound like:

- "What about what I want?"
- "What about how I feel?"
- "I thought about it, and I decided against...."
- "I can't take this anymore."
- "**You** made **me** feel like........"

When selfishness creeps in, it unlocks the door for divorce. A selfish spouse is the enemy's workshop. He will always discourage "us" by promoting "me." He will then give you sensible reasoning to justify being selfish. You may think to yourself that you have made many sacrifices for your wife, but now it's time that you do something for yourself even though she is against it. Oftentimes, when one spouse is against the wishes of another spouse, it is because that spouse's wishes are a threat against the marriage or a threat against the person. If the enemy is not exposed and cast out of your home, divorce will begin to look better than your wife.

Understand that the Bible refers to the unbeliever as blind. They are walking in darkness because they cannot see the obvious. The Bible refers to JESUS as the Light; therefore, in HIM, we won't be ignorant of Satan's devices. For this reason, the enemy tries to seduce the believer into having an adulterous relationship with "self."
When you start to give your flesh what you want, and when you spend too much time thinking about what you need, you will slowly start to love yourself more than you do your

spouse. GOD spoke against this in the book of Ephesians.

Ephesians 5:23-31 reads:

- "Husbands, love your wives, even as Christ also loved the church, and gave himself for it;

- That he might sanctify and cleanse it with the washing of water by the word,

- That he might present it to himself a glorious church, not having spot, or wrinkle, or any such thing; but that it should be holy and without blemish.

- **So ought men to love their wives as their own bodies. He that loveth his wife loveth himself.**

- For no man ever yet hated his own flesh; but nourisheth and cherisheth it, even as the Lord the church:

- For we are members of his body, of his flesh, and of his bones.

- For this cause shall a man leave his father and mother, and shall be joined unto his wife, and they two shall be one flesh."

When Divorce Looks Better Than Your Wife

Why did GOD command husbands to love their wives as they love themselves? Because marriage is ministry, and ministry is marriage. A Godly marriage reflects the fruit of the Spirit, and they include: love, joy, peace, longsuffering, gentleness, goodness, faith, meekness and self-control. Our marriages are a direct reflection of our relationships with the FATHER. HE loved us so much that HE gave HIS only Begotten Son for our sins. HE wants us to have that very same love for one another, but HE knows that selfishness threatens the sanctity of marriage.

Any time divorce starts to look like the better option, it is because the fruit of the Spirit was not present in that marriage; instead, the fruit of the flesh was present. As husbands, we often oppose the wrong things. Wives do this too, but we have to take responsibility for every open door in our marriages since we are assigned as guardsmen of our unions. When you see divorce on the horizon, the better thing to do is pray and ask GOD to reveal the devil behind your desires. Could it be pride? Is it jealousy? What about selfishness? The only time divorce will start to look good to a believer is when the flesh has revealed its hideousness. In many cases, divorce is not the answer; repentance is. Please understand that the fruit of the flesh doesn't just divide our relationships with our spouses; the fruit of the flesh acts as a divide between us and GOD. Being selfish is like playing Russian Roulette with a loaded pistol; there are no winners. As husbands, to be selfish means to refuse to cleave to our wives because we are too occupied with embracing ourselves. It means to exit the will of GOD to enter the will of the flesh, and this is not where we need to be.

When divorce looks better than your wife, it could only mean that you have been blinded by self. It means to leave the light of truth to walk in darkness. When divorce looks better than your wife, it is because you have fixated your eyes on something else or someone else, even if that someone is you. You forgot to love your wife as you love yourself; therefore, your love for her decreased as your love for yourself increased. You became so consumed with yourself that you didn't realize you were being devoured. Now, it goes without saying that if the wife has committed adultery, you have the right to seek a divorce, but that's up to you and GOD. Nevertheless, irreconcilable differences simply mean that a demonic strongman came into your home and kicked you out. Instead of binding up that devil, you started dining with it.

Any time divorce is an option in your marriage, you need to seek a stronger faith in GOD. Divorce is a mindset, not just an act. It is an ungodly doctrine, and just like every other ungodly doctrine, it derived from the Word of GOD taken out of context. JESUS proved this when the Pharisees questioned HIM about divorce. *"The Pharisees also came unto him, tempting him, and saying unto him, Is it lawful for a man to put away his wife for every cause? And he answered and said unto them, Have ye not read, that he which made them at the beginning made them male and female, And said, For this cause shall a man leave father and mother, and shall cleave to his wife: and they twain shall be one flesh? Wherefore they are no more twain, but one flesh. What therefore God hath joined together, let not man put asunder. They say unto him, Why did Moses then command to give a writing of divorcement, and to put her away? He saith unto them, Moses because of the hardness of your hearts suffered you to put away your wives: but from the beginning it was not so. And I say unto you, Whosoever shall put away his wife, except it be for fornication, and shall marry another, committeth adultery: and whoso marrieth her which is put away doth commit adultery.*

His disciples say unto him, If the case of the man be so with his wife, it is not good to marry. But he said unto them, All men cannot receive this saying, save they to whom it is given. For there are some eunuchs, which were so born from their mother's womb: and there are some eunuchs, which were made eunuchs of men: and there be eunuchs, which have made themselves eunuchs for the kingdom of heaven's sake. He that is able to receive it, let him receive it" (Matthew 19:3-12).

You will notice that the Pharisees asked the LORD if it was lawful to divorce one's own wife for "every cause." Of course, "every cause" means "any reason." Basically, they were divorcing their wives for what we now refer to as "irreconcilable differences." And they tried to justify this by reminding JESUS of the law in which Moses gave the people. Isn't that what we do today? A man who wants a divorce will find any excuse to justify his reasoning. The issue is that he is dwarfed by the responsibilities of marriage, and pride has become his Delilah. Even though his eyes are open, he is blind to the obvious. All he sees is Delilah's beauty, because that's all he wants to see. His eyes aren't open to the truth until they've been put out, but by then, it's oftentimes too late. He'd committed adultery against his wife with his own pride, and he soon found out that pride only sought to expose him and have him destroyed. *"Pride goes before destruction, and a haughty spirit before a fall" (Proverbs 16:18).*

When Divorce Looks Better Than Your Wife

Every disagreement you have with your wife is a chance to develop. It is an opportunity to grow stronger, get wiser and gather more understanding. In school, we had to go level to level, and each level was harder than the previous one. Fifth grade was more challenging than the fourth grade; tenth grade was more challenging than the ninth grade, and college was more challenging than high school. Each level prepared you for the next level. That's what disagreements do. When disagreeing, you have the opportunity to apply the knowledge you've received from the Word of GOD. If you have no knowledge, you'll fail the test. This is why we absolutely have to have the Word in us before we can impart longevity into our marriages.

If divorce is on your menu, take the time out to repent and reflect. Instead of reflecting on the issues you had, reflect on the roots of those issues, and then reflect on the Word of GOD. Was the Word applied in your marriage? What could you have done differently? Are you spiritually eligible for a divorce, or have you allowed the hardness of your heart to become your marriage's gravestone? Is there another woman vying for your attention, or have you started an adulterous relationship in your heart that you want to entertain? Sometimes, the best thing to do is reflect on our own wrongs, because many arguments aren't a reflection of our spouses' imperfections; they are a response to our own.

Our Story

There were many times that I considered divorce. There is one particular time that I remember the most. The relationship between Connie and I was breaking down, and we could never agree on anything. If I said "up", she said "down". If I said, "Now is the time to move," she said, "Not yet. Wait on the Lord." One day, we traveled to my parents' house (Freddie and Dorothy Cole) in Beckley, West Virginia for the holidays. The trip was eight hours long, and even though we had our children in tow, we didn't say much to each other. We only spoke when stopping for gas or bathroom breaks. When we arrived at my parents' house, they were quite naturally glad to see us. They were especially happy to see what they lovingly referred to as their "grandbabies." We stayed a couple of days with them and tried to enjoy the holidays, but the thickness between us was obvious.

One night, my dad asked me to take a ride with him. We left, and while I did the driving, he asked me, "How are things between you and Connie?" At that, I began to tell him that I did not feel Connie and I were going to make it much longer. In fact, that was the very reason I brought the grandchildren for them to spend time with because I'd planned to file for divorce when I got back to North Carolina. My father spoke a word into my life that I will never forget. He said, "Your mother and I have been married for over thirty-six years. Things have been good, and sometimes things got bad. I mean real bad! Do you think that I have never thought about leaving her? Every man can reach that point, but Godly fathers and husbands do not have this option because of the vows we made to God at our weddings. I would be lying if I told you that it would always be easy, or that you will always know what to do for your family. But, I can tell you that if you allow Jesus to be in the center of your marriage and your life, the Lord will bring you through." He ended by saying, "You can do what you want, but if it were me, and I had a loving wife like Connie and those beautiful and healthy children, I would stay right there. God's got a plan for your life as head of the house, and blessings for Connie and the kids that you can't see right now. I would stay and protect what God has given me. Just wait and see. It will be alright."

Those words were enough to convict me and encourage me. I stayed with my wife and twenty-seven years later, I have not regretted it for one day. Remember this: Don't divorce your wife; divorce yourself so that you can remarry your wife every day until your vows are fulfilled.

Fruit of the Spirit Versus Fruit of the Flesh

It is very important to not only know what the fruits of the Spirit are, but to understand the ingredients therein. It is equally important to understand the fruits of the flesh so that we can avoid them. In this chapter, we will discuss the fruit of the flesh and the fruit of the Spirit.

Love: Love is the most important ingredient in marriage, but the problem nowadays is that people have redefined what love is and what love does. Love is not an emotion. Love is Spirit, for GOD is love. *"And we have known and believed the love that God hath to us. God is love; and he that dwelleth in love dwelleth in God, and God in him" (1 John 4:16).*

Joy: Joy is the infilling of GOD; it is the

evidence that one's faith is made whole and doubt is not found in them. Joy is our spirit's response to the presence of GOD.

Peace: Peace is resting in the promises of GOD. To have peace is to have faith, for one cannot have peace without resolution. The absence of faith is found in the presence of conflict.

Longsuffering: Longsuffering is patience, and this is what most believers lack. No marriage can survive without longsuffering, for longsuffering is believing GOD through the tests of time, no matter what challenges your faith. Longsuffering is not to suffer long with the spouse; it is to suffer yourself not to be moved at the presence of adversity. Remember, adversity comes from the adversary, the devil.

Gentleness: This is one fruit that often gets tossed out when adversity comes on the scene. The problem is that we often forget that our wives are spirit beings; therefore, we keep coming at their flesh with our flesh. If we learned to see one another as GOD sees us, we would learn to be almost as gentle as HE is. *"A soft answer turneth away wrath: but grievous words stir up anger" (Proverbs 15:1).*

Goodness: For goodness sake, we have to be good to our spouses. But we can never be good husbands when we are not great sons of GOD. To be good means to choose right over wrong, faith over fear, and unity over individuality. It means to choose to do what GOD says simply because you love HIM. If you choose to do right for any other reason, you are wrong, and your right is selfish. *"If ye love me, keep my commandments" (John 14:15).*

Faith: Hebrews 11:1 defines faith this way: *"Now faith is the substance of things hoped for, the evidence of things not seen."* To have substance means to be inwardly filled. Faith is to be inwardly filled with the Word of GOD. *"So then faith cometh by hearing, and hearing by the word of God" (Romans 10:17).* Faith is to believe GOD in spite of your situation. Just as without faith we cannot please GOD, without faith our marriage reports won't please GOD.

Meekness: To be meek is to have understanding of what you are and Who GOD is. It is to be humble, and not self-boasting, self-driven or self-seeking. To be meek is to take one's eyes off self and place them on GOD. It is to look up and realize that you are down. Meekness is spiritual jewelry. *"But let it be the hidden man of the heart, in that which is not corruptible, even the ornament of a meek and quiet spirit, which is in the sight of God of great price" (1 Peter 3:4).*

Self-Control: Proverbs 25:28 reads, *"He that has no rule over his own spirit is like a city that is broken down, and without walls."* What does it mean to be like a city without walls; a city that is broken down? A city without walls is always open for invasion. It absolutely has no defense against its enemies. Self-control is to wear the armor of GOD in the midst of your flesh.

Fruit of the Spirit Versus Fruit of the Flesh

The fruit of the Spirit is absolutely critical to the survival of a marriage. Anytime one of these fruits is not present, the fruit of the flesh will come on the scene, and the divide will begin like a crack in a windshield. What are the fruit of the flesh again? They are adultery, fornication, impurity, licentiousness, idolatry, witchcraft, hatred, strife, jealousy, wrath, selfishness, divisions, heresies, envyings, murders, drunkenness and revelings.

Adultery: Adultery is one of this nation's number one reasons for divorce. Adultery is one man or woman's desire or decision to fulfill the lusts of the flesh with another person other than their spouse. In adulterous relationships, lust takes the forefront of our lives, whereas love is placed in the backseat. Any time adultery presents itself in a marriage, it brings the divorce papers and a few demons with it.

Fornication: Fornication is the coming together of two unmarried souls for lustful purposes. Fornication means to commit illegal sexual acts against one's body using your own body. *"Flee fornication. Every sin that a man doeth is without the body; but he that committeth fornication sinneth against his own body" (1 Corinthians 6:18).*

Impurity: Impurity means to be contaminated by sin. It means to have an idolatrous relationship outside of GOD, or an adulterous relationship outside of your spouse. Any and every form of impurity is the entryway to a strongman that, if left unopened, will become a revolving door for devils.

Licentiousness: Means to be lewd and lascivious. It means to have an ungodly desire or commit an ungodly sexual act with another person. In the marriage setting, there are some acts that are considered lewd because they go against GOD'S purpose for each part of our bodies. Such acts feed the flesh and cause it to grow stronger when we are commanded not to follow after the lusts of the flesh.

Idolatry: Idolatry is the worship of idols, or

reverencing another person or thing as your god. This can be done directly or indirectly. Idolatry not only threatens our relationship with GOD, but it threatens our relationship with every one of the blessings that GOD has given us. One can have an idolatrous relationship with their spouse, for example. This is done when a person loves their spouse more than they love the LORD. When the order of GOD is not followed, divorce is inevitable.

Witchcraft: Believe it or not, witchcraft is very common in marriage. How so? Witchcraft isn't just the casting of spells; witchcraft is to use ungodly tactics, wiles or devices to obtain something from someone else. It is to use trickery. For example, manipulation is witchcraft. Many people use divisive tactics to override their spouse's will, but this is ungodly, since GOD gives us the right to say "yes" or "no." Matthew 5:37 warns us this way: *"But let your communication be, Yea, yea; Nay, nay: for whatsoever is more than these comes from evil."* Using anger to get what you want is manipulation; therefore, it is witchcraft. Using tears to get what you want is manipulation; therefore, it is witchcraft. The proper thing to do is give the spouse the flexibility of saying "yes" or "no" without the threat of repercussions. After all, GOD says that vengeance is HIS.

Hatred: Hatred is self-worship. It is the very opposite of GOD, for GOD is love. Hatred means that one has cast judgment in their heart as if they were GOD. It is the very nature of Satan, for he desires to be GOD. To hate someone means to envy GOD and oppose the works of HIS hands (people or a particular person). It is the very opposite of GOD, for hatred is akin to murder, whereas CHRIST JESUS is the Way to everlasting life. Hatred starts to brew in marriage when one or both parties stops acting loving towards one another.

Strife: Strife doesn't mean to disagree; it means to take the disagreements to heart. Strife is one of the main ingredients of hatred, and strife is the wife of unforgiveness. If allowed to conceive, strife will birth out every evil thing in your marriage. That's why GOD commands us not to let the sun go down on our wrath. HE knows that if given more time, strife will begin to birth out devils.

Jealousy: Jealousy means to be emotionally moved by the accomplishments of another person. Jealousy is also having a self-entitlement mindset. When one is jealous about their spouse, their jealousy is only justifiable if the spouse commits adultery. Anytime unjustifiable jealousy enters a union, reasonable thinking exits the marriage and strife moves in.

Wrath: To have wrath means to be extremely angry at another human being to the point where you become vengeful. Vengeance is an act of GOD that should never be touched by a mere man. GOD'S wrath is justifiable, and HIS judgments are just. Man's wrath is rarely justifiable and never just. Wrath is toxic to a marriage, even in small doses.

Fruit of the Spirit Versus Fruit of the Flesh

Selfishness: To be selfish is to be totally and completely unlike GOD. Selfishness is the granddaddy of hatred and the stepfather of every other sin in existence. Selfishness is self worship. It is taking one's eyes off GOD'S will to indulge in self will. A selfish person honors himself/ herself above GOD. It means to disregard GOD, HIS angels and HIS people for one lone person: yourself.

Divisions: Any divide in the home is of the enemy. To be divided means to be self-conscious and self-driven. GOD called man and his wife one person, and HE made it very clear that only HE could divide a man from HIS wife. *"What therefore God hath joined together, let not man put asunder" (Mark 10:9).*

Heresies: A heresy is a belief in a doctrine that opposes the Word of GOD. It is basically to believe what Satan said over what GOD said. If you believe another doctrine, you cannot cover your wife, nor will you follow the Word of GOD when it refers to the responsibilities of a husband. To believe any report other than

Fruit of the Spirit Versus Fruit of the Flesh

GOD'S report is to be in total enmity with GOD.

Envy: To envy someone is to covet who they are. It means to disregard who you are and what you have because you have an ungodly infatuation (lust) after the identity and possessions of another human being. To envy someone is to murder them in your heart. *"Ye lust, and have not: ye kill, and desire to have, and cannot obtain: ye fight and war, yet ye have not, because ye ask not" (James 4:2).*

Murder: Of course, murder means to take the life of another human being. Murder isn't always a physical act, nevertheless. Hatred and envy are directly linked to murder.

Drunkenness: GOD calls us to be sober-minded. To be sober-minded means to have thinking unaffected by drugs, alcohol, people, doubt or fear. An intoxicated mind is one that's too busy to think about or consider the Word of GOD.

Revelings: To revel in something is to indulge

in it. It is the act of finding extreme pleasure and satisfaction in material things or situations.

As husbands, we have to literally memorize the fruit of the Spirit and the fruit of the flesh. In doing so, we will always recognize the force behind our choices. We will also be able to recognize what spirit is in operation in our homes and in our marriages. If it's not the Spirit of GOD, we know to bind it up. In learning these fruits, we are actually taking self-defense and marriage-defense classes. We are learning to discern the enemy and fight for the survival of our family units. During a disagreement, this knowledge will help you to make the right choices on behalf of your family. You see, when the truth lives in you, you'll become calmer. Anytime you're overly emotional, it's because confusion is chasing you and fear has cornered you. Remember, a man full of the Word is a man of few words. He simply speaks the Word, and GOD'S got it from there!

Divorcing Yourself to Marry Her

Every man commits bigamy against his wife with himself. Sometimes, he loves himself more than he loves his wife. Sometimes, he thinks more about what he wants as opposed to what is necessary for the betterment of "us." One day, he's trying to give his wife what she wants and needs, and on other days, he has to go and pacify self. When neglected for too long, self starts to whine about everything a man does for his wife and how it's not being done for self. For this reason, we have to constantly divorce self to marry and remarry our wives every day.

There was a time when Connie, and I were on a budget that I did not want to cooperate with. I felt I should be able to buy whatever I wanted without consulting Connie. I wanted a new car, but the budget did allow for it at the time. I could have gone ahead and purchased a car without talking it over with Connie, but she'd already warned me of excess spending. Nevertheless, I knew I could pay for the car, and the payments seemed like no big deal to me. I could have done it, but I decided not to because I'd promised Connie I would not make any large or major purchases without us first talking about it and praying to God for direction. I was at the dealership, but conviction weighed heavily on my heart, so I told the salesman I would have to come back after I talked with my wife. You know this was no easy feat, considering I really wanted to purchase a new car, and I had a reasonable-sounding salesman churning away at my thoughts. What's the purpose of this story? I'm reasoning with you as a man to a man. I could have purchased that car. I could have dishonored the agreement that my wife and I had made. I could have defended my right to have what I wanted over what we'd agreed upon. I chose not to, because the price I would have had to pay for such a decision was far greater than any money I had access to. In making the purchase, my wife would have lost trust in me, and she would have felt that her position in my heart was not a stable one. The wrong decision could have opened up the door to strife, unforgiveness, lack of trust and possibly ended our marriage. In that instant, I had to make a choice to divorce myself to marry my wife again.

Every day of our lives, we are given the right to choose our directions, but it doesn't mean we always make the right choices. That's why GOD sent HIS only Begotten Son to live and die for us. HE is our reconciliation to GOD, but we have to divorce our flesh every day to recommit ourselves to GOD every day. After all, the flesh is there when we wake up in the morning, and it is often the first voice we hear. The flesh is a nag, and it doesn't like to be reasoned with. It wants what it wants, when it wants it. For this reason, GOD told us to submit our bodies to HIM. Romans 12:1 reads, *"I beseech you therefore, brethren, by the mercies of God, that ye present your bodies a living sacrifice, holy, acceptable unto God, which is your reasonable service."* Therefore, to stay in right-standing with GOD, we have to come against our flesh. Our flesh isn't just our bodies; our flesh is the desires of our bodies and our natural minds.

Just as we have to divorce our flesh and submit it to GOD, we have to divorce selfishness to stay committed to our wives. There will be times when you know you need to discuss something with your wife, but pride will tell you that you are the man. Pride will tell you that you don't need her permission for anything, but you cannot listen to pride. Instead, you have to rebuke pride and come against your flesh's lustful desires to follow after pride.

Every day, you are meeting your wife at life's altar to remarry her all over again. There will be days when you will go on the lamb, and there will be days when you will happily accept your role as her husband. But you have to remind yourself that you have to divorce yourself for GOD anyway. Why not just utilize that time to learn to walk after the Spirit? *"This I say then, Walk in the Spirit, and ye shall not fulfil the lust of the flesh. For the flesh lusteth against the Spirit, and the Spirit against the flesh: and these are contrary the one to the other: so that ye cannot do the things that ye would" (Galatians 5:16-17).* Just as your flesh is against the Spirit, your flesh is against the wife, unless the wife is submitting to its lusts. That's because the flesh is selfish.

To remain married, you have to divorce you every day of your life. Does this mean you won't get what you want? Not at all. As a matter of fact, you will find that the more selfless you are, the more your cup will overflow with the blessings of GOD. After all, HE knows what you want. HE said that HE would give us the desires of our hearts and HE said HE would give us what we asked for. **Psalms 37:4**- "Delight thyself also in the LORD; and he shall give thee the desires of thine heart."

1 John 3:22- "And whatsoever we ask, we receive of him, because we keep his commandments, and do those things that are pleasing in his sight."

James 4:2- "Ye lust, and have not: ye kill, and desire to have, and cannot obtain: ye fight and war, yet ye have not, because ye ask not."

Matthew 7:7- "Ask, and it shall be given you; seek, and ye shall find; knock, and it shall be opened unto you."

Remember, selfless husbands die to self to live for GOD. In doing so, their selfish desires are snuffed out and replaced with Godly desires, and every one of those desires are filled in overflow. Stay married to your wives, not yourselves.

Training Your Mind to Forgive

One thing about forgiveness is it's not an option for the believer. We absolutely have to forgive our brethren, and we absolutely have to forgive our spouses. Oftentimes, we don't enter unforgiveness when someone sins against us one time; we enter unforgiveness when someone repeatedly offends us, or when someone touches our "soft spots." We often don't have a problem forgiving those on the outside of our homes because they don't have continued access to us to repeatedly sin against us. If a friend offends us, we simply end the friendship if the offense merits it. If a co-worker offends us, we simply avoid them from here on out. But when the wife offends us, we have to enter new territories of reasoning, because our wives have around-the-clock access to us to repeatedly offend us and touch our "soft spots". We are constantly exposed to our wives, even when there are wounds that need time to heal. In marriage, healing can never be a lengthy process; otherwise, bitterness may set in. Healing must be pursued from the moment hurt sets in.

Forgiving a spouse isn't as easy as it sounds. Now, when your marriage is new and still bordering perfection in your mind, forgiveness is effortless because you don't have enough evidence to make a case against them. But once you get to know your spouse and their hang-ups, forgiveness may take longer to process because they are already convicted (in your mind) of being selfish, inconsiderate, argumentative, unappreciative and stubborn. Once a conclusion has been drawn, we often draw from it and respond as judges rather than as spouses.

But how do you train your mind to forgive someone who has a license to offend you? It's simple: You train your mind to forgive: period. Forgiveness isn't a process, as many would have you to believe. Forgiveness is a choice that we make. GOD chose to forgive us, and HE sent HIS only Begotten Son to redeem us from the fiery clinches of hell. When CHRIST was nailed to the cross, HE chose to forgive those who were crucifying HIM and those who were mocking HIM. It was a choice that HE made. When your spouse offends you, you have two options: forgive them or don't forgive them.

The issue with most of us is we want to forgive, but we want to do it on our own terms. We think along the lines of, "If she will acknowledge that she was wrong, I will forgive her. If she would only apologize, I would forgive her. If she would give me what I want, I would give her what she needs." But forgiveness just does not work this way. The Bible basically tells us not to let anger spend the night with us. There is a reason for this, of course. *"Be ye angry, and sin not: let not the sun go down upon your wrath: Neither give place to the devil" (Ephesians 4:26-27).* The reason is that by allowing wrath to set up in your heart for too long, it eventually becomes unforgiveness, and unforgiveness is an iniquity. This means that you open up your heart for the devil to come in, and that's why he sows discord between you and your spouse. His desire is to divide, conquer and then devour the both of you. When you are angry with one another, you are like a microwavable dinner to the enemy. He hungrily stands by and enjoys the aroma of your feuding. He waits for the two of you to finally swell up with pride; this lets him know that you are almost ready. Finally, the haughty look comes when the heart has hardened; destruction of your marriage ensues, and the enemy starts enjoying his sanctified snack.

To train your mind to forgive, you must first understand the spiritual side of the human mind. Your mind is an information highway to your heart. Anything that gets into your heart must first enter your mind. When information first enters the mind, you have a choice:

receive it or block it. Anything you receive is granted access to your heart; anything you do not receive is kicked out of your mind, and another thought comes to replace it. Of course, anything that is stored in your heart will affect the way you perceive and treat your wife. That's why you'll hear some men say that they don't see their wives the same way anymore. What they are saying is new information has entered their hearts and removed the old information that once encouraged them to love their wives. Because they received these thoughts, their hearts were changed to house these new mindsets. First understand that the way you think is not stored up in your mind; it is stored up in your heart. The mind is simply the place where new ways of thinking come in, but the heart is where they are stored up. We don't actually say what we think, we say what we believe. *"A good man out of the good treasure of his heart bringeth forth that which is good; and an evil man out of the evil treasure of his heart bringeth forth that which is evil: for of the abundance of the heart his mouth speaketh" (Luke 6:45).* This tells that the battle isn't just to destroy our marriages; the enemy is always trying to change our hearts from good to evil. If he can get enough bad information past a man's mind and into his heart, he can change the texture of his heart and cause him to destroy his own marriage. At the same time, a man with a hard heart will destroy his life and ruin the lives of his children. This assault against the man is an assault against everything GOD has given the man, not just his marriage.

When a thought comes in, and it is a negative thought, you need to address it immediately. If it does not line up with the Word of GOD, it needs to be cast down. 2 Corinthians 10:5-6 reads, *"Casting down arguments, and every high thing that exalts itself against the knowledge of God, and bringing into captivity every thought to the obedience of Christ; and having a readiness to punish all disobedience, when your obedience is fulfilled."* What does this scripture tell us? Let's rightly divide the scripture.

"Casting down arguments and every high

thing that exalts itself against the knowledge of GOD." Of course, we know what arguments are, but what are the "high things"? Psalms 101:5 reads, *"Him that hath an high look and a proud heart will not I suffer."* The "high thing" in reference is pride. How does pride exalt itself against the knowledge of GOD? It's simple. Pride says, "I am right." GOD says, "I am Who I am." This is to say that there is none right but GOD. When a man puts on pride, he exalts himself against the knowledge of GOD. What is the knowledge of GOD? The knowledge of GOD is the already declared Word or doctrine of GOD. GOD is HIS Word, and HIS Word is GOD. *"In the beginning was the Word, and the Word was with God, and the Word was God" (John 1:1).* In exalting one's self against the knowledge of GOD, one exalts himself against the LORD.

We cast down arguments by not arguing. We have to have the Word in us to believe the Word, and when the Word is in abundance in us, the Word will flow from our hearts. When there is little to no Word in us, whatever we have in abundance in our hearts will flow into our marriages. Anything that takes the place of the Word of GOD is called impurity, or false doctrine. Doctrines aren't legal documents that have been officiated by man; a doctrine is any report introduced to man. A doctrine is a declaration; something designed to enter the heart of a man and change the way he thinks. False doctrine opposes the Word of GOD; therefore, it is designed by the enemy to evict GOD from your heart.

"Bringing into captivity every thought to the obedience of Christ." How does one pull off this feat? Remember, the Bible tells us in Ephesians 4:8 that CHRIST led captivity captive. What was this captivity that the Bible spoke of? Bondage. We were all slaves to sin, but CHRIST paid the ransom to set us free. Therefore, the Bible is telling us to put off the old man or old way of thinking and put on the new man in CHRIST. We have to put on the mind of CHRIST in our everyday lives and in our marriages. What did CHRIST tell us about marriage? If your thoughts don't line up with what HE said, arrest them and speak the Word to them. They have no choice but to obey!

"Having a readiness to punish all disobedience, when your obedience is fulfilled." How does one punish disobedience, especially in the marriage setting? Should you emotionally remove yourself when your wife is not acting right? Should you walk out of the house when she brings strife in? No. After all, you pay the bills in your house; therefore, strife has to go. You punish disobedience by making a declaration in your home; that is, you continue to do as GOD has instructed you to do, and you lead your house in this obedience. That's why the scripture tells you to be ready to punish all disobedience when YOUR obedience is fulfilled. That means that you can't correct someone when you need correcting. You have to practice what you preach.

The next time you and your wife do not agree, simply turn to the Word of GOD to see what GOD says about the matter, and then enforce that. Obeying the Word of GOD should not be an alternative in your house; it has to be law. As the head of the house, you are there to enforce the law. There is no negotiating with the Word; either you and your house will serve it, or you won't. Let's say, for example, that your wife has a son from a previous relationship. Since he is not your "blood" son, she does not want you to discipline him. Instead, she wants to be his disciplinarian or let his "blood" father discipline him. How would you resolve this? It's simple. You are her son's father, just not by blood. You are feeding him, training him and providing somewhere for him to stay; therefore, do what the Word says a father ought to do with his children. If your wife opposes this, don't back down. Try to speak with her about the issue, but continue to do what GOD told you to do.

You train your mind by feeding it the Word of GOD every day, until the Word rests in your heart and flows from your life. When you feel unforgiveness in your heart, evict it with the Word. The Word of GOD cannot dwell alongside unforgiveness. Someone can remember the scriptures, but this does not mean that they believe what GOD said. It simply means they "remember" what GOD said. You have to believe GOD in order to receive the blessings of GOD. Here are a few tips to train your mind to forgive:

1. Be willing to forgive. This is the first step you have to take. Someone not willing to forgive has chosen to remain in unforgiveness.

2. Don't attach demands to your forgiveness. Just rightly forgive, even when the person doesn't deserve it. After all, this is what GOD did for us.

3. Find at least one scripture that relates to your dispute, and follow it. Instead of confronting or reprimanding your wife, go to the scriptures to see what GOD has to say.

4. When your wife is not willing to budge, hand the situation to the LORD and leave it there. Don't put your hands back on that situation; instead, let GOD change you and your wife for HIS glory.

5. When angry thoughts haunt you, don't flee from them; confront them.

Remember to confront every thought with the Word of GOD, and bring every thought unlike GOD into captivity.

6. Say "I love you" even when you don't feel it. After all, love isn't a feeling; love is Spirit. Be humble with your words and let love do what it does!

7. No two marriages are just alike. Please do not compare someone else's wife to your wife. Always remember that people act one way in public and another way behind closed doors. Besides, the Bible tells us not to be jealous of what someone else has. The grass always looks greener on the other side of the fence, but it still has to be mowed.

8. Everything changes over time, but it is not always for the worst. This is why we have to have an anchor that we hold on to when the storms of life arise. Remember and tell yourself: 1.) "I can do all things through Christ that strengthens me." 2.) "Trouble does not

last always." 3.) "This too shall pass."

9. Consider your reasons to love her. Sometimes, we forget why we love our spouses when they have taken us beyond our limitations. Try telling her the reasons you love her as opposed to the reasons you dislike her sometimes. Remember, a soft word turns away wrath.

10. Just say it. Say, "I forgive you" when strife enters the room. The quickest way to make a devil run is to obey GOD. *"Submit yourselves therefore to God. Resist the devil, and he will flee from you" (James 4:7).*

You have total control over your own mind, because GOD gave you "free will." Free will is the ability to move like GOD and make decisions as a god; therefore, you have power over whatever thoughts attempt to enter your mind. You wouldn't let the neighbor's kid walk through your front door without knocking, head to your kitchen and start making himself breakfast, right? The same goes for your thoughts. Don't let a foreign thought come into your mind without GOD'S permission, head into your marriage and start cooking up drama. Speak to your mind. You have the power to tell you how to think. Insanity is when one relinquishes authority over their own minds, and it becomes invaded with wrongful thinking and false doctrine. Don't let the enemy run you crazy in your marriage and then convince you that peace can be found outside of your marriage. If he's successful in his attempt, you will find what millions of divorcees have found out: craziness follows the crazy one, no matter who they marry!

Changing the Atmosphere In Your Marriage

As the head of the house, you control the atmosphere in your marriage. Sure, the atmosphere can be affected by an argumentative wife or rebellious children, but at the end of the day; it's charged to you to get and keep your home in order. As men, when we decide to get married, we oftentimes aren't aware of the responsibilities we will have, and by the time we get this reality check, the vows have been exchanged, and there is no turning back. You can't just divorce your spouse because you don't want to learn or adapt to your new role. You have to confront your fears and let go of your normal to embrace your newest assignment.

Changing the Atmosphere in Your Marriage

Over the years, you will find that there will be days when you come home to a peaceful and loving home. Everyone will be joyous, and your wife will be passing out smiles. Then there will be the days when your house looks like a haunted house. Everyone in the house will be grumpy, and your wife won't look like the meek woman you married. Instead, she will be unfamiliar and negative. The worst days are usually the ones when you are in a great mood, and you come home to a negative environment. Days like that are oftentimes the days that our reactions are heightened because of expectation. Since the day went great at the office, we expected the day to be even better when we got home. Instead, there was a force in our homes that hid behind the door as we entered. This force ambushed our joy, slaughtered our peace and started trying to bind us. As you can imagine, this force is oftentimes demonic.

As the heads of our homes, we should always be sensitive to the environment in our homes. This is how we know when we have an unwelcomed guest, and we will know when the LORD is present. Show me a man who does not know his family or the feel of his home, and I'll show you a man who's living with demons.

When we are calm, this usually indicates that our homes are being run as usual. Everyone is their normal selves, and everything goes as scheduled. But there are those times when you can sense something in the atmosphere. Your wife may be in a good mood and your children may be in a good mood, but you can still sense something in the atmosphere. Something's just not right at home, and even though you can't put your finger on it, you are spiritually and consciously aware that something is out of place. Think about a blind man who lives alone. Amazingly enough, he can usually get around his house without tripping over any furniture. At the same time, if someone was to enter his house, he would be more sensitive to their presence than a man with sight because he has learned to depend on his other senses. At the same time, he is more sensitive to his environment because this is a mechanism GOD gave him to survive. Sadly enough, a large number of husbands are spiritually blind to the point where they can't see the obvious. They only recognize the moods of their wives and children, and they respond to their moods and not what's triggered their alarms.

Once we get married, we aren't just husbands. We have to take on and master so many titles, including provider, protector, warrior, lover, friend, helper and leader. Anytime we slack in any one of our roles, the enemy will use that door to attack our families. We have to always be sensitive to the sound of doors opening into our spirits and our homes. But this new generation of husbands is so sensitive in the flesh that they are spiritually numb. What's the verdict then? How can we learn to be aware of and change the atmospheres in our homes? It's simple. We have to be sensitive to the HOLY SPIRIT. HE will make us aware of any changes that occur in our homes, in our persons and in our marriages. At the same time, we have to know our families, and we have to know the feel of our homes. We need to recognize when our atmospheres have been altered and when there is an unholy presence in our homes, so we will know to put on the full armor of GOD and cast anything unholy out. Sometimes, you'll be able to detect a shift in your atmosphere before the enemy finishes sowing his seeds, and because of this, you'll cast him out, uproot his seeds and close off any demonic access doors into your home. A man who is serious about his position as a leader and a covering for his family is a man the enemy fears.

Satan likes to distract us with so many cares of the world so that we won't take the time out to learn the temperature of our marriages and when there is any change in the temperature of our marriages. *"And the cares of this world, and the deceitfulness of riches, and the lusts of other things entering in, choke the word, and it becometh unfruitful" (Mark 4:19).* As you can see from the scripture, the cares of the world will uproot the blessings in our lives if we allow these things to come in. What are the cares of the world? They include fear, worry, doubt, frustration, anxiousness, depravity and so on. For example, when our bills are Goliaths and our bank accounts look like Davids, we often fear that our Goliaths will prevail against us. Sure, David overcame his Goliath by believing GOD, but the average believer thinks his giant is far greater than David's giant. Because of this, many come to the battlefront covered with armor that's too big for them and carrying around a sword that's too heavy for them. What they should have done was walked out as they are and used the Sword of the Spirit. The cares of this world are temporal; therefore, they invoke the temporal man or flesh.

But let's say that the atmosphere of your home has been chaotic, to say the least. You've thought about leaving your own home in search of a better environment. Here's a word for you: Don't leave your home, change your atmosphere! How can you cause a shift in the atmosphere of your marriage?

1. Love your wife despite her flaws. You

do this by forgiving her time and time again and speaking softly to her, even when your flesh is telling you to speak otherwise.

2. Honor your wife as the weaker vessel.

3. Speak to the atmosphere. It has to obey you when you command it in JESUS Name.

4. Stand together with your wife against anything demonic. Don't stand with demons against your wife.

5. Get any and everything demonic out of your house and destroy it. Out of ignorance, many couples have decorations, souvenirs and fixtures that represent other deities, and these items give demons permission to enter your home.

6. Be mindful of what you watch or allow to play on your television set. Also be mindful of the music you listen to and allow to be played in your home. Every word spoken is full of seeds, and if you allow evil words to be sown into your

mind, it's only a matter of time before they grow up in your heart.

7. Be mindful of who you allow in your home. Let's face it. Some people have devils attached to them, and their devils follow them everywhere they go.

8. Express your love for your wife and children every day. They shouldn't go one day not hearing you say that you love them, and they shouldn't go one day wondering if you love them.

9. Keep your children in order. Rebellious children invite spirits into your home, because rebellion is a spirit. Discipline your children, cast rebellion out, and keep your house demon-free.

10. Pray every day with your family. A short prayer can change the course of a long day.

11. Ask your wife to join in. After all, she is your help meet. Your wife is still a leader in the home; you are just the head. There will be times when you are not on the job, but your wife will be. Set

some rules in place for the running of your home, and make sure that you and your wife are in agreement.

12. Exercise and eat right. Sometimes, the food we eat encourages and discourages our moods.

13. Keep the house clean and uncluttered. A dirty house always has a negative atmosphere.

14. Put up a "no trespassing" sign for vengeance. There will be times when your wife will upset you, but you should never take it upon yourself to take revenge against her. Revenge includes leaving the house for long periods of time, being argumentative, emotionally starving her or refusing to eat food she's cooked. Also talk with your wife and the two of you should come to a mutual understanding that vengeance will not be a part of your marriage.

15. Keep secrets out, and always be open with one another. An untold secret can stress your spirit man to the point where

your wife will detect the presence of something in you, but she won't know what it is. In cases like this, she may become insecure, fearful, emotional or angry. Just tell her the truth at all times, even when you are uncomfortable doing so.

16. Laugh often. A home full of laughter is a home full of joy.

17. Get out of the house sometimes. Most women want the opportunity to get beautified and go somewhere they've never been before. Grant your wife this pleasure as often as you can.

18. Manipulation and sarcasm are pride's guests. Don't invite them into your conversations or dealings with one another.

19. Leave random love notes around your house at any given time. You can write ten a month and just hide them throughout the house. Over the months and years, your wife will find those notes. There will be days when she's

not so happy with a decision you've made, and one of those notes will be found by her. That note will cause a shift in her heart and in your day.

20. Let GOD be GOD. Realize and recognize that there are some things you just can't do. Give it to GOD and keep on living.

Always remember that the atmosphere of your home is a manifestation of what is going on in your heart. Change what's on the inside of you so that that when your life opens up, the wrong things won't come out of it.

Changing the Blueprint of Your Marriage

Everyone has a mental draft of what a marriage is. Most women started their drafts at a relatively young age. Most men look at the marriages of others, and when they see a union that appears to be sound and stable, they use that marriage as a blueprint for what they want. When husbands and wives unite as one person, they bring their drafts, and both parties start trying to build what they believe to be a good marriage. Oftentimes, men take it day by day. They focus on what happened today, what happened yesterday and how we can prevent it tomorrow. Women, on the other hand, focus more on next week, next year, the next five years and even on a lifetime. So what you end up with is two people with two separate visions of what a marriage is, and both parties keep ripping each other's blueprints up to start their own. Marriage then becomes a competition that both parties strive to win. Let's review three rounds of common issues in a marriage, and we will discuss how each round knocks us out of GOD'S will.

Round One- Round one involves a husband whose idea of marriage is going to work, coming home, enjoying great food, year 'round physical access to the wife, two children, access to unlimited privacy and his favorite sports. That's as far as he's thought, and that's his blueprint for marriage. In the other corner is a wife with big dreams. Her idea of marriage is to have the big house on the hill, three children, three luxury cars, date night once a week, a marriage full of loving gestures and the infamous talk once or twice a week to remove any negative energy that's crept into the marriage. She doesn't believe in privacy because she believes that both parties should be together at all times.

The bell rings, and they are at one another's throat once again. The wife is hurt because her dreams are for the betterment of the marriage and their lifestyle. Her vision is to have a marriage structured around the emotional highs of being in love and growing together as a family unit. Her vision for growth involves the weekly meetings, the plans to move into a new home and she wants to terminate anything that comes in with negative energy. Her plan isn't bad, but it doesn't involve what the husband wants because she believes she has covered everything already.

The husband is angry because all he's asking for is peace. To him, everything is going just fine as it is, so why is she not content with her life? His children are happy, he can afford the monthly rent, his job is stable and he's got food on the table. To him, he is an overachiever because he has gotten everything on his wish list plus some. To him, the wife is the problem because she is acting as a threat to what they have trying to pursue what she wants. In his mind, she is coveting what others have, not understanding that the people she's trying to pattern after are struggling financially, their marriage is on the rocks and their children are half past crazy.

Both parties come forth with their demands, prepared to fight it out, but in this round, pride slithered up behind both of them and took the victory. Both parties had visions of staying together, but they had differing views on what is, was and should be done. They should have taken it day by day, not giving place to the thoughts of tomorrow. *"Take therefore no thought for the morrow: for the morrow shall take thought for the things of itself. Sufficient unto the day is the evil thereof" (Matthew 6:33).* When the Word of GOD steps in, pride runs out, and the Word claims the victory. Everyone standing on the Word is more than a conqueror through CHRIST JESUS.

Fight Stats: Both parties are right, and both parties are wrong. As men, we want to provide for our families, and when we find a comfortable setting where we can do so, we don't want to be moved. After all, any move we make may threaten our plans. What if we move into a bigger house and can't afford it? How do after school activities help our children? To us, these activities are more for the Mom than the children. It's just a mother who wants to live vicariously through her children, and she wants to prove something to someone. Maybe it's those family members who doubted her and spoke failure over her life and the lives of her children. In other words, women are often moved by faith, but their faith isn't always grounded in GOD. They have faith in themselves that they can be the best super-soccer moms. Men, on the other hand, are oftentimes grounded by fear. When we are comfortable, we are at peace. It took us too long to find this peaceful place, and we don't want anyone trying to move us from it. Therefore, the way to resolve this issue is to come against pride, fear and doubt. Both parties should have come together to draw up a blueprint that fits what they both want, allowing room for what they won't get. The problem is oftentimes that neither party is willing to negotiate or come to the table with a negotiation. Both parties want what they want, and they'll battle it out to get it until divorce steps in to separate them when the fight gets too vicious.

Round Two- The husband's plans for his children are that they go to a public school, make good grades and be obedient children. He's not focusing on what they will become as of now; he's focusing on keeping them fed, keeping a roof over their head, and making sure they do what they are told to do. He wants to keep everything simple because he wants to come home and enjoy his family every day. He wants to have meals every day scheduled at six-thirty in the evening, where the family sits together in the dining room to discuss their days.

The wife's plans for her children are that they go to a private school, make good grades and be obedient children, but with room for error. She wants her sons and daughters to be successful, so she is involving them in many after school programs and activities to keep them busy. She is focused on their futures to the point where she is busying herself with their day-to-days. Any threat to her plans for them is met with hostility. She doesn't have time to prepare a meal every day at six-thirty because the children have after school activities that they are into. She has to pick them up with no help from her husband, and she oftentimes spends half of an hour to an hour chatting it up with other mothers who she befriends at these after school locations. Most of the meals that she prepares are frozen meals and processed foods, and these meals are thrown together around eight-thirty or nine o'clock in the evening. There is no fixed schedule.

The fight starts, and the husband is upset because he doesn't have his definition of a wife, and the wife is upset because she does not have her definition of a husband. To the wife, the husband should be more active in his children's activities, and since he's home around five in the evening, he could easily cook a meal. To the husband, the wife is being unreasonable, and she's obviously watched too many episodes of the Cosby's.

Both parties come to the forefront to fight it out, but again, in this fight, pride makes its way into the ring to claim yet another victory.

Fight Stats: Both parties are very wrong. The

wife is sacrificing the opportunity to develop a strong family bond for whatever fear, lust or desire is driving her. Her vision for her children is a good one, and it's how mothers think. She wants her children to be overachievers, and this desire is oftentimes rooted in self or fear. It could only mean that the wife has an opinion of what success is and how to arrive at it that the husband does not share.

The husband is wrong because he's not investing much into his children's futures. His desires to be monotone are more than likely rooted in selfishness, fear and the lack of vision. Sure, we should never take any thought for tomorrow; however, we should utilize the power of today to build foundations for a better tomorrow.

One way this issue could have been resolved is by giving both parties what they want, but first fear, envy, selfishness and blindness should be bound. The wife didn't have to involve her children in so many activities. After all, when you trust the LORD with your children, you won't have to do everything in your own might. The way to change a child's future is to change their minds. This could have been done at home, without sacrificing the opportunity to eat lunch together as a family unit. At the same time, both parents could have agreed to educational family outings to occur weekly or bi-weekly. There are two scriptures we need to consider here to keep our families together and keep strife from becoming members of our families.

Amos 3:3- *"Can two walk together, except they are agreed?"* It's Word, and its official. If the two of you cannot agree, you won't be able to accompany one another in this thing called life; therefore, you have to come to a mutual understanding for the sake of staying together. Two people fighting to have their own way will eventually part and go their own ways.

Luke 11:17- *"But he, knowing their thoughts, said unto them, Every kingdom divided against itself is brought to desolation; and a house divided against a house falleth."* This scripture basically joins hands with Amos 3:3. Your house won't survive the winds of change if the two of you are not grounded in the Word of GOD. Let GOD lead your homes, and peace will then come to live with the both of you, but as long as you are having selfish and pointless quarrels that get you nowhere, peace will be still outside of your home. Peace is always still, but when you don't invite it in, it'll go be still somewhere else.

Round Three- The children of the couple are now teenagers and pre-teens, and they are all going through their rebellion stages. The daughter is sixteen years old, and she believes she is mature enough to date. The mother agrees, but the father does not. Having once been a sixteen-year-old boy, he tries to protect his daughter from the raging hormones and bad decisions of a young man. Their son is now thirteen years old, and he's addicted to video games. The father wants to leave him alone as he is. After all, in his line of reasoning, he isn't bothering anyone. The mother wants the father to place limitations on playing video games, and she wants him to spend more time with his son. Her vision of a father-son relationship is one where the father takes the son fishing, goes outside to play catch with him and takes him on long drives to discuss what it is to be a man. The father's vision of a father-son relationship is one where he's there to feed and discipline his son.

Finally, there is a twelve-year-old daughter who wants permission to talk on the phone with boys. The mother is okay with this arrangement because she feels it's harmless. After all, the boy won't have physical access to their daughter; nevertheless, to the father, mental access gives a young boy just enough pull to lead his naïve daughter into a place where he's granted physical access. The father stands his ground, and the mother covers her ground with thousands of words designed to move him from where he stands.

In this fight, there are no human winners, but pride takes the belt.

Fight Stats: Again, both parties are wrong. The husband is wrong because he is obviously not involving himself in the important discussions that relate to the rearing of the children; however, he is present to present his final decisions. The mother is wrong because she is not listening to her husband in relation to her sixteen-year-old daughter. In the days before the written Bible, men had to ask permission of the father to take his daughter's hand in marriage. Oftentimes, it was the family of the groom who asked the family of the bride. This means that their intentions were good. If a man was going to take his daughter away from him, he was prepared to cover her as a husband and provide for her and the children he may have with her. In these days, boys ask the girls permission to take them out on dates. These dates are no marriage proposals; instead, they are oftentimes opportunities for young men and young women to act as married people. A sixteen-year-old boy isn't looking for a wife, and daddy knows this. He's looking for a good time, and the father is trying to keep his daughter from being some boy's "good time." What the father is basically saying to his wife is, "Allow me to raise my daughter to be a respectable woman, so that when a man comes for her hand in marriage, he will do so the right way and when he's mature enough to know that she's more than an opportunity to get lucky. Let a man come along when he's ready to be a husband and she's ready to be a wife. Let us send our daughter to school and further educate her on the importance of loving and respecting herself. Until then, I don't want any boy near her because he's not going to return her to me deflowered and possibly pregnant with no intention to take care of what he created." In these cases, the wife is saying, "I know how my daughter feels. I was once sixteen years old, and I know the pressures of fitting in. Let us trust our daughter and not deprive her of what I believe to be a crucial and defining time for her life."

Again, the father was right to protect his daughter, but the mother's intentions were not wrong either; nevertheless, her decisions were rooted in the wrong things.

The father is wrong because he's being too lax with his son. Instead of taking the time out to groom him to be a man, he's allowing video games to instruct him. This is because the father is being lazy and doesn't want the added responsibilities that his wife is hoping he'll take on. Getting too comfortable is always an issue, since GOD keeps us on the move. When a person gets too comfortable, they are oftentimes unwilling to go through the open doors that lead to renewed minds and better lifestyles. Finally, with the twelve-year-old, the father is right once again, and the mother is wrong, because the father is trying to protect his daughter, whereas the mother is trying to negotiate with her.

Now, as a husband, you'll likely side with the man in all of these scenarios. Most women would likely side with the women, because men and women see things differently. That's a fact that can never be disputed, but how do you bring such conflicting views under one roof? It's simple. We have to come together with our wives to draw up a plan for our lives, and this has to be done immediately. Any time there is no blueprint on the table, there are no plans on the table. Instead, we will just follow the first idea that looks like a good idea each day, and this would lead us back to where we started. We have to draw up our blueprints based on the Word of GOD, and not on opinions and good ideas. The question we have to repeatedly ask ourselves is, "What would JESUS do?" We have to run our homes the way we know CHRIST would run HIS. We can't be moved by opinions and the fads of the day, because these things are temporal and lead to nowhere. We have to raise our families the way GOD has instructed us to do so, and that's when the blessings will be upon our homes.

Take time to schedule a meeting with your wife. Talk to her about every issue you think may present itself. You may have to have this meeting every day for a week until the two of you have pretty much covered every base you see the enemy will try to score on. Agree not to argue before the talks begin, and agree not to be offended with one another's opinions. In addition, agree to respect one another's views even when you don't understand them, and do not walk away from this meeting just because you feel you are not getting your way. After all, the whole point of the meeting wasn't to find a way to give you what you wanted; it was to meet at a new understanding, one in which GOD is the head. End each meeting on a positive note and maybe even take your wife out to eat a few times to show her that you appreciate her willingness to discuss each issue in a loving way. Be sure to include the following in your discussions to keep the atmosphere light:

1. Tell your wife that you love her and intend to spend your life with her. This removes fear in the case where the two of you can't seem to agree. It'll help her to relax and focus on the issue at hand and not on the direction of your marriage.

2. Take breaks when necessary. Sometimes, you can sense that the communication is taking a wrong turn. Politely and respectfully take a break to focus on something positive before returning back to the discussion.

3. Don't be so eager to speak, but also be willing to listen. Request that your wife do the same.

4. Always bring pen and paper so you can jot down your proposals and your agreements.
5. Let GOD be seated at the head of your discussions, and make sure you are doing this for HIM. *"For where two or three are gathered together in my name, there am I in the midst of them" (Matthew 18:20).*

Making the Best of What You Have

The majority of us grew up poor. When we did have food to eat, we didn't have a lot of choices. We had to eat what we had and be thankful for it. Truthfully, not having a choice is never a problem when you're hungry. It's only when alternatives are present that we take too much time considering those alternatives and worrying about our choices. A poor man can't watch his diet. He has to eat what's available to him. The irony in this is hungry people don't complain when they get fed. They don't care if the bread is white bread or wheat bread. They don't care if you give them a chicken breast or a chicken wing. They just want to eat. Unfortunately, this cannot be said of marriage. We do have alternatives, and it doesn't matter how we look, how much money we have or how twisted our minds are, there are always women out there willing to accept us as we are. Therefore, staying married can be a challenge.

A lot of husbands take to relationships outside of their marriage units because the other women will receive them just as they are, but their wives keeps pushing them to change. What man doesn't want to be accepted as they are? Well, you shouldn't, and let me explain why.

When you get a job, your goal is to make money and to be promoted so you can make more money. There aren't too many men out there who don't want to be promoted on their jobs. The same goes in the realm of the spirit. Promotion is available to you, and sometimes the door of promotion is open, but it may look intimidating. Remember, the Bible calls the wife a help meet. Your wife will always encourage you to go through those doors of

Making the Best of What You Have

change. Even though her method of pushing you may be wrong, many times, her intentions are not. A woman who is not your wife will oftentimes see how frustrating this push is to you, and how you are rebelling against going through that door; therefore, she has no problem closing it for you. In this, she may appear to be the better person, whereas your wife may come off as being evil. That's because when a man is in the midst of an affair, he is spiritually blind and can't see the obvious. A blind man depends more on sound because he has no sight to depend on; therefore, a spiritually blinded man will listen to what a woman says because he can't see the truth. For this reason, a woman who appeals to you may be granted permission by you to contend with your wife spiritually. Make no mistake about this walk. It's not about your flesh; the devil is after your soul. When you involve yourself in an adulterous affair, you have chosen with your will to be bound, and the fight shifts from you covering your home to your wife trying to uncover your secrets. At the same time, your wife is then given the spiritual responsibility by you to come against every demonic spirit that has been set loose in your marriage. The issue then becomes you see an angry wife who keeps opposing you, and you see a friendly mistress who keeps justifying you. Which way do you turn? Most men won't leave their wives for their mistresses; however, they will consider separating from their wives to get full-time access to their mistresses. That's because the mistress has presented herself as a willing alternative to your wife, but your wife keeps presenting herself as an unwilling participant in your affair.

Most men who enter adulterous affairs feel justified in their decisions. Maybe the wife is too argumentative, or she's not submissive enough. Maybe the wife is pushing the man towards change when he wants to remain as he is. Maybe the wife isn't seductive enough, or she doesn't play by his rules. For whatever reason a man chooses to enter an affair, he has chosen to exit the will of GOD to pursue his own lusts. Every married man can give you more than one hundred reasons as to why he could cheat on his wife, but only a man grounded in the Word of GOD could give you seventy times seven reasons that he remains faithful to his wife. *"Then came Peter to him, and said, Lord, how oft shall my brother sin against me, and I forgive him? Till seven times? Jesus saith unto him, I say not unto thee, Until seven times: but, Until seventy times seven" (Matthew 18:21-22).* Whatever error he finds in his wife, he has to forgive her for it and love her past it. After all, that's what marriage is. Marriage is not trying on a person to see how well they fit into your life. Marriage is finding a way to break the molds that we have designed to fit into GOD'S will for us, even when it does not match our wills for ourselves. Marriage is reconciling with GOD'S will for our lives and for our marriages.

A garden starts off as nothing but dirt. The dirt has to be turned and the weeds have to be removed. No gardener ignores his garden. Instead, he plants beautiful flowers in it, he waters it and he fertilizes it. He prunes the dead leaves off his plants so that death won't spread to the roots of that plant. Every flower is precious to him. If his flowers aren't budding properly, he considers what he's done wrong, not what the flowers have done wrong. He changes his fertilizer, reads up on the proper care and maintenance for his garden, and he does whatever he believes to be necessary for the growth of his garden. Any foreign debris that gets into his garden, he will promptly remove. He is a gardener, and he takes his job seriously. No one has to tell him when his plants need water or the ground needs turning. No one has to tell him when one of his plants is not getting enough sunshine. He recognizes each bloom in his garden, and he cares for it with love. He doesn't consider his neighbor's garden because he has to take care of what belongs to him, not the neighbor. He makes the best of what he has. What about you?

Every year that your wife is with you, you should see growth in her because of what you impart into her. She is a precious seed that GOD has entrusted you with. If cared for properly, she will bud into a beautiful ornament in your life's garden. She will make you look good, and she will drop many new seeds in your garden. She was given to you by GOD to be cared for, nurtured, protected and watered. You should always encourage her growth in the LORD, and this is a job that you have to take seriously. Her life is in your garden. Anytime you see foreign plants growing up in her garden, you ought to remove it. GOD has given you the tools to help her prune that dead flesh off her so that it won't root itself in her heart. To properly care for her, you need to be educated. That's why GOD sent HIS Word to you, and you should study HIS Word every day of your life. You should be the first to know (besides GOD) when something is wrong in your wife. Instead of trying to create a new garden with someone else, you have to learn to make the best of the one GOD gave you. Sure, the enemy will offer you a beautiful garden that doesn't require much work, but what he won't show you is how that garden will work you over. When the blessings come from GOD, there are no curses attached to it, but this doesn't apply with Satan. *"The blessing of the LORD, it makes rich, and he adds no sorrow with it" (Proverbs 10:22).* GOD requires that you operate in love so Satan won't trap you with beautiful lies designed to seduce and destroy you.

Would you rather buy the house that you want or build the house that you need? There are so many people who end up selling their homes because they saw beautiful structures that they wanted to live in. Once they move into their new homes, they quickly find that even the very setup of that house is an inconvenience to them. Find a homeowner who does not like his home, and he will tell you that he spends most of his time in certain rooms, but there are certain rooms that he avoids altogether. So, even though he moved into a big house with all of the amenities, he lives in a studio apartment inside of his house. Eventually, he will either sell his house or stop paying the bills on it altogether because he's paying to live in a place that he's not happy with. Find a man who bought the house that he needed, and you'll find a happy man who keeps building on to his house. Eventually, he will have the house that he wants and needs all stacked up in one. What's the difference between these men? The first man was in a rush to enjoy a harvest that he did not sow. The second man was patient enough and wise enough to receive his blessing and serve as a blessing to his blessing. When two blessings come together, more blessings are born. The same goes for marriage. Over the course of time, if you build your wife up and refuse to tear her down, she will continue to grow up unhindered in CHRIST. At the same time, she will continue to bear fruits for you; fruits that will bless you and help you to come into the wholeness of who you are. GOD created us to be reciprocal creatures. When you bless the wife, she becomes a blessing to you. The same goes from the plants of this earth. We give off carbon dioxide to plants, and in return, plants give us oxygen. You can't get something for nothing, and even if you feel that what you're receiving does not match what you are giving, you may need to check the spirit behind your giving. Are you giving with expectation, or are you giving in love?

Everything in the realm of the earth starts off as a seed and is elevated to a harvest once it has undergone the necessary growth process. This includes our marriages, ourselves and our spouses. Sometimes, the process takes longer for others than it does for ourselves, because we may be resisting change rather than embracing it. The good wife you have right now is a seed away from becoming a better wife tomorrow. You are a good seed right now who will emerge as a Godly harvest later if you stay in CHRIST. Every seed requires work, and if you take care of the garden GOD has given you, in time you will reap a bountiful harvest. Don't look at another man's wife and wish you had her. Don't look at other women and allow the enemy to convince you that they could be better for you than your wife. Always remember that GOD gave the man the responsibility of "toiling" the ground. This means that man has to work all the days of his life. "Toiling the ground" doesn't just represent having physical fields where you grow crops. We are under a new covenant, so "toiling the ground" is now spiritual. You have to sow, and then when the season is upon you, you have to reap. Keep sowing good seeds into your marriage until you reap the marriage that you want.

Adultery Stats and Revelations

Scientists and stat centers have conducted years of research on the study of both women and men. While these statistics aren't always accurate, they do border accuracy and confirm what GOD has been saying all along. In this chapter, we will review the results of some studies and elaborate on the findings.

DIVORCE

The following below shows the **percentage of divorces in the United States by age**.

Age	Women	Men
Under 20 years old	27.60%	11.70%
20 to 24 years old	36.60%	38.80%
25 to 29 years old	16.40%	22.30%
30 to 34 years old	8.50%	11.60%
35 to 39 years old	5.10%	6.50%

Stat Reference: www.divorcestatistics.info

Conclusion: We all know that adults under the age of twenty-years-old are, for the most part, still in a selfish state of thinking. That's why they are the largest group of party-goers in the United States. They are also more likely to be involved in a traffic accident than older age groups, because at that time in their lives, their minds have not yet matured. Consequentially, when they enter marriage, they are less likely to stay married because they are still new to themselves as adult.

As we get older, we are more likely to stay married because the big picture presents itself to us as we get over ourselves to embrace life. Ironically enough, these statistics show the world's findings, but they can be loaned to the church since the church's stats are no different.

Also, consider the spiritual side of this. When we are young in the faith, we are more likely to divorce because we have not yet matured in the LORD; therefore, it is never wise to marry when your faith is not yet made whole.

Matthew 6:33- *"But seek you first the kingdom of God, and his righteousness; and all these things shall be added unto you."* We know that Abraham believed GOD, and it was counted to him as righteousness. This tells us that in order for us to seek the kingdom of GOD and his righteousness, we have to believe GOD. How can you believe what GOD said if you don't know what GOD said? Any man who does not know the Word of GOD is not fit to marry, since marriage is a GOD-ordained institution, and marriage is ministry.

As you grow older in the LORD, getting to know HIS Word, you will begin to mature and, in due season, GOD will entrust you with a wife.

Divorce Rates After First, Second and Third Marriages

"The marriage breakup rate in America for first marriage is 41% to 50%; the rate after second marriage is from 60% to 67% and the rate in America for third marriage are from 73% to 74%." **Stat Reference:** www.divorcestatistics.info

Conclusion: Stay married to the first one if you can. The likelihood that you will divorce increases for every marriage you enter. A lot of people think that divorcing one person to marry another will increase their chances to have happier marriages, but the only chance that is increased is the likelihood for divorce. Divorce often comes into the picture because of one or two selfish people; nevertheless, divorce is not a cure for selfishness. Instead, divorced parties grow increasingly selfish, bitter and demanding, thus the reason for their increased chance for divorce. Please note: Just because the "other woman" smiles at you from the outside doesn't mean she'll keep smiling once she's on the inside. She's actually more likely to not trust you than your wife because of how she got with you. Even when there is no "other woman", you are responsible for your wife, and you are still accountable to GOD for the vows you have made. You might as well make the best of it instead of straining it more because you're not getting what you want out of it.

Malachi 2:14- *"Yet ye say, Wherefore? Because the LORD hath been witness between thee and the wife of thy youth, against whom thou hast dealt treacherously: yet is she thy companion, and the wife of thy covenant."*

Remember, the world can divorce you with their laws, but if GOD has not separated the union, you are still married to the first one; therefore, any other marriage you enter won't work.

Mark 2:9- *"What therefore God hath joined together, let not man put asunder."*

INFIDELITY

The stats below show infidelity stats and their marriage survival rate after infidelity.

Adultery Stats and Revelations

- 69% of marriages don't survive an affair.
- Studies suggest that only 31% of marriages make it through infidelity.
- 80% of couples who get divorced after an affair regret the decision.
- 17% of divorces in the United States are caused by infidelity.
- Research suggests that 56% of divorces are caused by an obsession with pornography.
- Weight loss surgery patients have an 85% greater chance of divorcing their spouses.
- Studies suggest that 75% of married couples with special needs children get divorced.

Men. Vs. Women

- Recent studies suggest that there is infidelity in 8 out of 10 marriages in the United States.
- 68% of women in the United States say they would have an affair if they knew they would never get caught.
- 74% of men say they would have an affair if they knew they would never get

caught.
- 54% of married men do not know that their wives are involved in extramarital affairs.
- Studies suggest that 70% of married women do not know their husbands are having an affair.
- 14% of married women in the United States admit to having had an affair.

Cheating Types and Results:

- 12% of Americans spend up to ten hours a week looking for sexual encounters online.
- 44% of married men cheat because they feel they are not having enough sex in their marriage.
- 40% of married men who have an affair use an escort service.
- 64% of adults believe that sexting can be an act of infidelity.
- Research suggests that almost three percent of all children are the product of infidelity.
- Studies show that 75% of relationships

which start out as affairs end in failure.
- 10% of adulterers eventually marry their lovers.

Stat Reference: Oprah.com

Conclusion: GOD'S Word will never and has never returned to HIM void. There is no way around HIS Word. Some of the stats that stick out the most are:

69% of marriages don't survive an affair- You are more likely to lose your wife in an affair than for any other reason under the sun. Here's what's fascinating, however. **80% of couples who get divorced after an affair regret the decision**. This tells us that it's simply not worth it even when we think it is. The **31% survival rate** of marriages impacted by infidelity is also an alarming number because it indicates that forgiveness is not exercised in marriage, even though marriage is supposed to be ministry.

Research suggests that 56% of divorces are caused by an obsession with pornography- As men of GOD, we know that we should not watch pornography because we are the temples of the HOLY SPIRIT. The Bible tells us to guard our hearts. *"Keep thy heart with all diligence; for out of it are the issues of life" (Proverbs 4:23).* Truth be told, 100% of men who watch pornography will have an affair or multiple affairs. Why is this? Adultery starts in the heart, and then it manifests in the body. *"But I say unto you, That whosoever looketh on a woman to lust after her hath committed adultery with her already in his heart" (Matthew 5:28).* You have a wife. Enjoy her and forbid your flesh from leading you into sexual sin and causing you to be at enmity with GOD.

68% of women and 74% of men say they would have an affair if they thought they would not get caught- This fact of the world is awful, and I can only hope that this is not the truth for the church. This tells us that this world is becoming increasingly dark because the people are becoming increasingly selfish and against the LORD.

12% of Americans spend up to ten hours a week looking for sexual encounters online- There is a spirit on the loose, and it is luring the men and women of GOD into sexual sin.

There, the enemy plans to devour them, but first, he will destroy their marriages, pervert their children and tear down their minds. Again, GOD told us to guard our hearts, for out of it flow the issues of life. Everything you allow into your imagination is going to shape, affect or destroy your life. You have to make a conscious decision not to indulge in pornography or adultery. Don't let this spirit into your homes.

44% of married men cheat because they feel they are not having enough sex in their marriage- As men of GOD, we have to encourage our wives in the faith every day. We have to read to them what the Word of GOD says so that they won't withhold themselves from us. At the same time, we need to find out how we are contributing to the lack of sex in our marriages. Oftentimes, it's due to pornography or something the husband has done, and then there are the times when it's because the wife has something hiding in her heart. Regardless of what it is, we have to seek the root of the issue and not cause other problems by trying to go outside of our marriages.

Studies show that 75% of relationships which start out as affairs end in failure- You can't win for losing, literally. You won't gain a better wife by losing a good one. Instead, selfish men pull selfish women, and these relationships just don't work.

Matthew 19:9- "And I say unto you, Whosoever shall put away his wife, except *it be* for fornication, and shall marry another, committeth adultery: and whoso marrieth her which is put away doth commit adultery."

Matthew 18:21-22- "Then came Peter to him, and said, Lord, how oft shall my brother sin against me, and I forgive him? till seven times? Jesus saith unto him, I say not unto thee, Until seven times: but, Until seventy times seven."

Proverbs 5:18-21- "Let thy fountain be blessed: and rejoice with the wife of thy youth. Let her be as the loving hind and pleasant roe; let her breasts satisfy thee at all times; and be thou ravished always with her love. And why wilt thou, my son, be ravished with a strange woman, and embrace the bosom of a stranger? For the ways of man are before the eyes of the LORD, and he pondereth all his goings."

Proverbs 6:26- "For by means of a whorish woman a man is brought to a piece of bread: and the adulteress will hunt for the precious life."

2 Corinthians 10:5- "Casting down imaginations, and every high thing that exalteth itself against the knowledge of God, and bringing into captivity every thought to the obedience of Christ."

1 Corinthians 7:5- "Defraud ye not one the other, except *it be* with consent for a time, that ye may give yourselves to fasting and prayer; and come together again, that Satan tempt you not for your incontinency."

1 Peter 3:7- "Likewise, ye husbands, dwell with *them* according to knowledge, giving honour unto the wife, as unto the weaker vessel, and as being heirs together of the grace of life; that your prayers be not hindered."

Is adultery fun? Yes, adultery will be fun when your heart is full of sin. But the consequences are far greater, and they are simply not worth it.

Adultery Stats and Revelations

It's like working a job for fifteen years where you know you have benefits and a hefty retirement plan, but quitting that job to start all over somewhere else where the only benefits you have are short-term. Is marriage fun? Yes, marriage can be fun, but marriage is also work. You will determine how much fun your marriage is and how much work you are willing to put into it. If you'd invested one million dollars into building materials to construct a house for yourself, you wouldn't give up on that house, no matter how hard of a task it proves to be. Your marriage is worth more than earthly riches, and there is no woman on the outside that can take the place of the woman GOD has blessed you with on the inside. Consider these facts:

- Any woman willing to have an affair with you is immoral and selfish. There's a reason that she's single. If she's married as well, she's giving you a preview of what it is to be married to her.

- Any woman willing to have an affair with you is likely bound by the souls of other men. Why trade your wife for another man's whore?

- Women who engage in adulterous affairs often have low self-esteem, even when they appear to be confident. Women with low self-esteem don't make for good wives.

- More than 50% of the women who will offer themselves to you as a mistress are currently involved in other sexual relationships.

- If you'll risk a spiritual union for a natural (fleshly) union, you are indeed carnal-minded, self-seeking and against GOD. Remember, the price David paid for Bathsheba was way more than any of us would be able to pay and retain our sanity.

- Sex inside of the marriage union can be far more gratifying than sex outside of it. Outside relations only encourage the work of the flesh; marriage encourages the work of the heart.

- Love is always better than lust, for GOD is love. When you love your wife, it means that GOD is with you and your wife. When you lust after another woman, it means you have abandoned GOD to seek your own glory. Always remember that Satan seeks anyone he can devour; therefore, when you enter sin, Satan is waiting for you with his fork in hand.

- Every tear your wife cries is counted by GOD, and you will give an account for every one of them that was caused by you. GOD entrusted you with her so that you could bring her joy all the days of her life. Don't do the opposite.
- Love never fails.

Staying Together to Tell the Story

One of the reasons divorce is so prominent today is there aren't many believers who stay together to tell the story. Fifty percent of marriages end in divorce. This isn't just in the secular realm; this is also a fact for the church. Because of this, there aren't many couples to look up to or look to for counsel. Instead, more and more young couples are finding themselves being mentored by thrice divorced individuals who make marriage sound like a roll of the dice. Many people end their marriages because they want to explore their chances to do better, but better just doesn't exist without faith. Without faith, marriages rarely survive.

Let's face it. No marriage is flawless, because

the people in the marriage are full of flaws. The problem with most people is they tend to magnify the flaws of their spouse while minimizing their own. We tend to place more expectation on our spouses than we do ourselves, and this is a recipe for an unhappy marriage. We are flawed, and our spouses are flawed. Over the course of my life, I have met many married individuals who were on their second or third marriages; sometimes more. In most of these cases, the divorcees had to marry multiple times before they accepted the obvious: no one is perfect, not even themselves. When you are married, it is so very easy to focus on what you are not getting when you are hungry in those areas, but it is not easy to pay attention to what you are getting because you're not lacking in those areas. Only after divorce and remarriage do many individuals come to the realization that one spouse may be great in one area of their lives, whereas a different spouse may be great in other areas. It's like having a bag of water that's full of holes. If you stop covering one hole to stop the other from leaking, you haven't made any progress; you're just moving your fingers around. That's what most people do. They move their bodies around by marrying other people, but their minds stay in the same places. They enter marriage behind marriage with a blueprint of what they want in a spouse. During the stages of marital development, they don't like what they see, so they abandon their marriages looking for a spouse who is a perfect match to their blueprints. What they don't realize is they've just torn down what they have built with one person, and they now have to start all over again with a different person.

But what if you stayed together? After all the storms and storm chasing; after all of the threats of divorce, the tears and the insanity; just what if you stayed together and it worked out? What if the two of you stopped fighting progression and agreed to do the will of GOD? What if the love was restored, the wounds were healed, and the wrong words were canceled and replaced by good ones? What if GOD cleaned the both of you up and started you all over again as newlyweds in HIS will?

Staying Together to Tell the Story

What if you honeymooned in CHRIST for the rest of your lives? Would you stay then? Most people would agree to stay, but they'd add on that they couldn't see their stubborn, insensitive, self-centered, insecure spouses ever making this transition. That's because we tend to focus on the flesh so much that we give up on GOD. The things that are impossible with man are possible with GOD.

The marriage union is a sacred one. It is holy ground. When Moses went to Mt. Horeb (the mountain of GOD), an angel of GOD told him to take off his shoes because he was on holy ground. Why did he command Moses to take off his shoes? Moses had undoubtedly walked through some unholy places; therefore, his shoes were defiled. When Aaron's sons Nadab and Abihu offered strange fire to GOD, they were immediately killed because they approached the Most Holy GOD in an unholy way. Before the Levites would enter the temple of GOD, they had to be consecrated. To be consecrated means to be "set apart." What does this mean to the marriage union? This means we have to be set apart from the world in our thinking. We have to approach marriage the same way we approach GOD. We have to realize that we are treading on holy ground when we get married. GOD refers to our wives as our crowns, and HE also gives us favor because of them. We have to be careful how we approach our wives, and our wives have to be careful how they approach us.

Any time a believing couple stays together, they glorify GOD with their decisions. They are the reason that doubters believe. One married couple who passes the tests of time will be an encouragement to many married couples who are considering throwing in the towel. Because of this, GOD will favor their union, bless their union, and protect their union. They are living examples that irreconcilable differences are not justifiable enough to pardon someone from their vows to GOD. They have pushed past many obstacles; they have considered or maybe even filed for divorce at some point during their marriages, but they loved past their hurt feelings. They went against all of the forces that threatened to divide them, and they crossed over into many decades with their hands still interlinked. They argued, they cried, and they walked out the door with no plans to return, but there is just something about love that kept bringing them back together once again. They've prayed for their unions, and they have prayed against their unions, but GOD saw them through every trial. HE wanted to teach them to love as HE loves. HE wanted to teach them about love, for love is the very essence of who HE is. *"Love is patient and kind. Love is not jealous or boastful or proud or rude. It does not demand its own way. It is not irritable, and it keeps no record of being wronged. It does not rejoice about injustice but rejoices whenever the truth wins out. Love never gives up, never loses faith, is always hopeful, and endures through every circumstance.*

Prophecy and speaking in unknown languages and special knowledge will become useless. But love will last forever" (1 Corinthians 13:4-8/ NIV). Let's rightly divide those scriptures. **Love is patient:** Love has to be patient; after all, GOD is love. How can HE deal with the wickedness of mankind if HE was not love? GOD is calling us to be like HIM, for without love, we are the complete opposite of who HE is. *"He that loveth not knoweth not God; for God is love" (1 John 4:8).*

Love is kind: GOD is kind to us. HIS love and kindness are the very reasons HE pardoned us from our sins. We couldn't approach HIM in the wrong way. We have to approach HIM in love; therefore, HE requires us to approach everyone else in the same manner. At the same time, animosity is the opposite of kindness. It is the very nature and behavior of hatred. *"A soft answer turneth away wrath: but grievous words stir up anger" (Proverbs 15:1).*

Love is not jealous: How can love be jealous? If your spouse was promoted at work, and you weren't; why would you become jealous, seeing that you will benefit from her promotion as well? Jealousy is the behavior of the self-righteous. You have to remember that Satan was jealous of GOD, and this is what got him kicked out of Heaven. GOD doesn't want you to act like Satan in your marriage.

Love is not boastful: Boasting is a representative of selfishness and pride. It is the evidence that the boaster has erected themselves as an idol in their own hearts. Because they are individually wrapped up in their own self, they can't see the greater picture of unity that GOD has created.

Love is not rude: We already discussed that love is kind, but here, the scripture mentions to us that love is not rude. Let's say your wife has offended you, and her words have cut you pretty deep. Now, you're being rude to her as a show of your disdain for her choices. What you are doing is taking revenge against her. Revenge isn't always a physical act that's carried out. Revenge can be choosing not to act in love towards one another with the intention of punishing the offending party. We have no right to be vengeful. *"Dearly beloved, avenge not yourselves, but rather give place unto wrath: for it is written, Vengeance is mine; I will repay, says the Lord" (Romans 12:19).*

Love does not demand its own way: Now, this is where a lot of married couples fork off, because the individuals in the marriage have the wrong definition of love. They have developed their own selfish doctrines of what love is, and any time someone goes outside of "their" love's boundaries, they become wrathful. Love is not selfish, but love sees the whole picture. That's why GOD said HE would give you and me the desires of "our" hearts. HE'S not a selfish GOD. Understand that our desires aren't always HIS desires for us; nevertheless, HE loves us so much that HE gives us what we want. We have to be the same way with our spouses. They may not make the right choices, or do the things that we want at all times, but we have to love them past it. If your love's limitations don't stretch outside of yourself, you will end up by yourself, for yourself, because of you!

Love is not irritable: How many times have we had a bad day and have taken it out on our wives and children? How many times have we allowed ourselves to become so emotionally sensitive that we couldn't even stand the sound of laughter or bear the sight of a smile? That's a heart issue, and it should never be taken out on our families, because those are not the acts of love. They are the acts of self-righteous thinking, whereas our attitudes become inflamed when we don't get what we want or what we think we deserve. That's not godly behavior; that's behavior that signals that we need to get on our faces before the LORD and release wrath before it turns into hatred.

Love keeps no record of being wronged:
Now, we can understand why the divorce rate in America alone is so high. Most married folks keep mental records of their spouses' wrongdoings. The most foolish quote alive is the most common one, and it is: "I can forgive you, but I won't forget!" This means that the person offended is keeping files in their hearts of their spouses' imperfect choices. Yet, we go before the LORD and ask HIM to forgive us for our sins, because we know that HE loves us, and HE is willing to forgive us. Can you see how this hypocrisy offends the LORD? If GOD can forgive us for our sins, and cast them away into the sea of forgetfulness, who are we that we can't do the same? Are we more righteous than GOD? Do we deserve more love, respect and honor than the Most High GOD? *"He will*

turn again, he will have compassion upon us; he will subdue our iniquities; and you will cast all their sins into the depths of the sea" (Micah 7:19).

Love does not rejoice about injustice but rejoices whenever the truth wins out: Under no circumstances is love unjust. What if another man's wife was to rob a bank, and the bank's teller happened to be your wife? The bank robber is apprehended, and your wife is the key witness at the trial. Because the video tape of the robbery isn't very clear, the jury decides that your wife's eyewitness account isn't enough to convict the woman who robbed her. At the sound of "not guilty" you hear a roar come out from the offender's husband. He rejoices at the sound of injustice being done. He laughs and rejoices while your wife is heartbroken. How would you feel? Now, imagine the bank robber was your wife. Injustice is injustice; fair is fair, and you should never be moved to quote otherwise. When your spouse is guilty of a crime against another person or a crime against the LORD, they have to be held accountable for their actions.

Without accountability, a human will continue to offend, and they may have hell to pay for their choices. Even if you are guilty of committing a sinful act against your wife such as adultery, and your wife believed your lie when you said you'd been faithful, you are not only being deceptive when lying to your wife, but you are rejoicing in injustice. That's why GOD tells us to confess our sins to one another. A person who confesses their sin is less likely to repeat the offense again.

Love never gives up, never loses faith, is always hopeful, and endures through every circumstance: Where is your love pointed? Any time we love ourselves more than we love our spouses, we won't give up on ourselves, but we will give up on our marriages. That's why you have to be mindful of the direction your love is pointed. When you become so wrapped up in yourself that your individual problems are greater than the issues in your marriage, you have totally disconnected yourself from GOD. After all, GOD is not going to worship you.

In addition, we have to remember

longsuffering. Longsuffering doesn't mean that you've suffered long enough; longsuffering means to endure. GOD told us to endure until the end. The issue with us is that the world told us we have options. We don't have to endure the behaviors of our wives because divorce is a few hundred bucks away. But this is not the heart of GOD. HE wants us to keep the faith and don't let hope die. Instead, believe GOD can change your spouse; HE can change you, and He can change the direction of your marriage. HE can, but you can't.

Love will last forever: How is this? How can love last forever, even after we have passed on? It's simple. GOD is love and HE is eternal. Even after a divorce, the love will still remain. That's why many divorced people don't fare well in other relationships. After divorcing, many people come to the realization that they could have worked out their marital problems; their issues weren't that big after all, and love doesn't divorce the two once it links them. Instead, love continues to link their hearts, even while they go on to enter other relationships. Loving from another from a distance doesn't fix any problems; oftentimes, it creates a void.

Why is it important that we know the behaviors of love? So we can know when we are not acting in love. We need to know when to correct ourselves. GOD wants us to hold our families together so we can tell the stories about how we survived one another, but more than that, how we survived ourselves. After all, we can be our worst enemies; nevertheless, we can't divorce ourselves, so we endure being who we are. We strive to change those areas we believe that need to be changed; we walk away from friendships that we believe are hindering our lives, and we even quit our jobs so we won't lose our minds. We do whatever we can do to make ourselves happy. This is exactly what GOD wants us to do for our spouses. HE wants us to treat them as we treat ourselves. We have to endure who our wives are but encourage a change in them when one is needed. We need to walk away from friendships that hinder our marriages, and we need to find jobs that don't send us to the brinks of insanity. That way, we won't come home and take that day's problems out on our wives. We need to always strive to be better than yesterday. When someone comes up to us to hear our stories, they should laugh, cry and be encouraged by what we say. People who were just about to give up should walk away feeling revived and ready to try GOD again in their marriages.

Nowadays, there are too many bitter souls out there who will happily tell our youth the things they did against their spouses before they divorced them. They tell these stories of drama where they have the starring role of right, and their spouses have the villain's role of wrong. In their stories, there is humor and horror, and each story ends the same way: they got divorced. They often come to life as they recall incidents where they felt disrespected, hurt or humored by their previous spouses' choices. No doubt, they enjoy this attention because they are kings and queens for the hour, in their sights. They still haven't realized that it was this drive for self that left them by themselves. Nevertheless, they are not shy about their stories, and some of their stories are so interesting that they could only be revered as the James Bonds of marriage. They were in and out of their marriages faster than the blink of an eye. What they don't share with these young adults; however, is that they are lonely and regretful of the choices they have made. They send away their audience with a mind full of foolishness to ponder. If given the change, they'd personally coach every last one of them out of their marriages as they attempt to recreate the scenes in their failed marriages that they believe caused their lives to come apart. Unhappy people have no trouble sharing their misery. This is why we are needed. We have to counteract all of the negativity that is sent out by these lost characters, the media and generational mindsets. Believe it or not, the survival of your marriage will save at minimum one marriage a year. Even when people don't say a word, they are still watching us.

Every good story pulls on every emotion

possessed by human beings. A good story triggers laughter, sadness, joy, energy, fear, faith, confidence and so on. A good story always involves a villain, and sometimes that villain is us; sometimes, it's our spouses. Every good story includes a hero, and with marriage, the Word of GOD is our hero. Every good story involves the threat of defeat, but it ends with reality of victory. We have to make it past all of the drama to get to the happy endings that GOD has promised us. We can't always be the heroes, either. We are more often the foes than we want to be, but we have to admit defeat so that GOD can declare victory. We have to admit our wrongs to show that GOD is right, because every good story comes with twists and turns that stun the viewers. You see, when GOD entrusts us to minister to other couples, they have to be aware of the fact that they aren't always right; even when both people oppose one another, there is still another side of the story that isn't being told. That side is GOD'S version of the story. I may say that my wife was being selfish with her requests that I put away my cell phone while we were on a date. My wife may say that I was showing no interest in her by sending text messages while we were on a date. But GOD may say that the both of us were acting like heathens because we were both so wrapped up in what we wanted, that we were led by our flesh into a long and drawn out argument, and that argument took us absolutely nowhere. We wasted precious time graced to us by GOD arguing about something we could have easily talked about. We put JESUS on hold so that we could three-way the devil into our marriages when we felt that he had a better solution as to how we could handle our spouses.

But we know better, so we have to do better. My wife and I survived because we learned that no matter how much we hated one another's ways, we loved each other far greater. At the end of a bad day, we still have the night to make it right. As we tell our stories, we both wonder how we survived together more than two decades, but it was only by the grace of GOD. Nevertheless, we don't regret our decision to stay together in the least. No other woman could put up with what my wife put up with, and no other man would have put up with what I had to put up with. That's because GOD gave us enough grace to extend it to one another. The presence of mirrors in our houses cast an imperfect reflection of us to ourselves, and the Word of GOD served as a spiritual mirror, casting an imperfect reflection of our hearts to us as well. How can imperfect me divorce imperfect her and hope to find the perfect woman? Only Satan encourages that lie because he knows that there is no such thing as the perfect man or woman. It's amusing to him to watch a man walk away from his marriage because he thinks he could create a better story with someone else. He watches as the lost soul enters relationship behind relationship looking for someone who could fit into his mental mold of the perfect woman. Satan laughs as this man's hopes are shattered again and again, and being blind, the man blames GOD for his choices. He did what many men do. He walked away from his marriage story, one that GOD wanted to author, to enter relationships that he wanted to author, and this just did not work for him or anyone else. We have to stay together in GOD'S will to tell the story HIS way.

__Scriptures Referencing Marriage__

Genesis 2:22-24- "Then the LORD God made a woman from the rib he had taken out of the man, and he brought her to the man. The man said, "This is now bone of my bones and flesh of my flesh; she shall be called 'woman, ' for she was taken out of man." For this reason a man will leave his father and mother and be united to his wife, and they will become one flesh."

Proverbs 5:18-19- "May your fountain be blessed, and may you rejoice in the wife of your youth. A loving doe, a graceful deer-- may her breasts satisfy you always, may you ever be captivated by her love."

Proverbs 12:4- "A wife of noble character is her husband's crown, but a disgraceful wife is like decay in his bones."

Scriptures Referencing Marriage

Proverbs 18:22- "He who finds a wife finds what is good and receives favor from the LORD."

Proverbs 19:14- "Houses and wealth are inherited from parents, but a prudent wife is from the LORD."

Proverbs 20:6-7- "Many a man claims to have unfailing love, but a faithful man who can find? The righteous man leads a blameless life; blessed are his children after him."

Proverbs 30:18-19- "There are three things that are too amazing for me, four that I do not understand: the way of an eagle in the sky, the way of a snake on a rock, the way of a ship on the high seas, and the way of a man with a maiden."

Proverbs 31:10- "Who can find a virtuous woman? for her price is far above rubies.

The heart of her husband does safely trust in her, so that he shall have no lack of gain.

She will do him good and not evil all the days of her life.

She seeks wool, and flax, and works willingly with her hands.

Scriptures Referencing Marriage

She is like the merchants' ships; she brings her food from afar.

She rises also while it is yet night, and gives food to her household, and a portion to her maidservants.

She considers a field, and buys it: with the fruit of her hands she plants a vineyard.

She girds her loins with strength, and strengthens her arms.

She perceives that her merchandise is good: her lamp goes not out by night.

She lays her hands to the distaff, and her hands hold the spindle.

She stretches out her hand to the poor; yea, she reaches forth her hands to the needy.

She is not afraid of the snow for her household: for all her household are clothed with scarlet.

She makes herself coverings of tapestry; her clothing is fine linen and purple.

Her husband is known in the gates, when he sits among the elders of the land.

She makes fine linen, and sells it; and delivers sashes unto the merchants.

Strength and honor are her clothing; and she shall rejoice in time to come.

She opens her mouth with wisdom; and on her tongue is the law of kindness.

She looks well to the ways of her household, and eats not the bread of idleness.

Her children arise up, and call her blessed; her husband also, and he praises her.

Many daughters have done virtuously, but you excel them all.

Charm is deceitful, and beauty is vain: but a woman that fears the LORD, she shall be praised.

Give her of the fruit of her hands; and let her own works praise her in the gates."

Deuteronomy 24:5- "If a man has recently married, he must not be sent to war or have any other duty laid on him. For one year he is to be free to stay at home and bring happiness to the wife he has married."

Matthew 19:4-6- "Haven't you read," he replied, "that at the beginning the Creator 'made them male and female,' and said, 'For this reason a man will leave his father and mother and be united to his wife, and the two will become one flesh' ? So they are no longer two, but one. Therefore what God has joined together, let man not separate."

1 Corinthians 7:1-16- "Now for the matters

Scriptures Referencing Marriage

you wrote about: It is good for a man not to marry. But since there is so much immorality, each man should have his own wife, and each woman her own husband. The husband should fulfill his marital duty to his wife, and likewise the wife to her husband. The wife's body does not belong to her alone but also to her husband. In the same way, the husband's body does not belong to him alone but also to his wife. Do not deprive each other except by mutual consent and for a time, so that you may devote yourselves to prayer. Then come together again so that Satan will not tempt you because of your lack of self-control. I say this as a concession, not as a command. I wish that all men were as I am. But each man has his own gift from God; one has this gift, another has that. Now to the unmarried and the widows I say: It is good for them to stay unmarried, as I am. But if they cannot control themselves, they should marry, for it is better to marry than to burn with passion. To the married I give this command (not I, but the Lord): A wife must not separate from her husband. But if she does, she must remain unmarried or else be reconciled to her husband. And a husband must not divorce his wife. To the rest I say this (I, not the Lord): If any brother has a wife who is not a believer and she is willing to live with him, he must not divorce her. And if a woman has a husband who is not a believer and he is willing to live with her, she must not divorce him. For the unbelieving husband has been sanctified through his wife, and the unbelieving wife has been sanctified through her believing husband. Otherwise your children would be unclean, but as it is, they are holy. But if the unbeliever leaves, let him do so. A believing man or woman is not bound in such circumstances; God has called us to live in peace. How do you know, wife, whether you will save your husband? Or, how do you know, husband, whether you will save your wife?"

Ephesians 5:22-23- "Wives, submit to your husbands as to the Lord. For the husband is the head of the wife as Christ is the head of the church, his body, of which he is the Savior."

Colossians 3:18-19- "Wives, submit to your husbands, as is fitting in the Lord. Husbands,

Scriptures Referencing Marriage

love your wives and do not be harsh with them."

Hebrews 13:4-7- "Marriage should be honored by all, and the marriage bed kept pure, for God will judge the adulterer and all the sexually immoral. Keep your lives free from the love of money and be content with what you have, because God has said, "Never will I leave you; never will I forsake you." So we say with confidence, "The Lord is my helper; I will not be afraid. What can man do to me?" Remember your leaders, who spoke the word of God to you. Consider the outcome of their way of life and imitate their faith."

Mark 10:6-9- "But at the beginning of creation God 'made them male and female.' 'For this reason a man will leave his father and mother and be united to his wife, and the two will become one flesh.' So they are no longer two, but one. Therefore what God has joined together, let man not separate."